PRAISE FOR *AGES OF ANXIETY*

An original and profound study of how war shaped Auden as a poet: how he used Jung's psychology to understand the turmoil and dread provoked by war, to organize morally and aesthetically the responses of the individual psyche and society to Fascism and to probe the poet's responsibilities in time of war. Today, as we again face wars, rising nationalism, and huge populations hungry for a leader to make them feel strong and safe, this nuanced, beautifully researched discussion is a contribution not only to literary scholarship but to understanding our own world.

—**Ruth Padel**, author of *Darwin: A Life in Poems,*
In and Out of the Mind, On Migration,
and *Tigers in Red Weather.*

A bold and multi-faceted re-visioning of Auden's neglected poetic drama of the mid-twentieth-century mind. Stephenson analyzes *The Age of Anxiety* in light of Auden's use of Jung's psychological types and assesses its impact on the Symphony that Leonard Bernstein based on Auden's poem and three ballets set to the Symphony. The author then weaves this impressive body of creative work into the history of the idea of *anxiety* from Kierkegaard through successive editions of the *DSM*—a startling achievement.

—**Austin Clarkson**, author of *On the Music of Stefan*
Wolpe: Essays and Recollections and *"My Mind a*
Beautiful Thing": Imagination, Art, Creativity in
Elementary Education.

In the current time of mounting political tensions, with dark echoes of escalating intolerance, Craig Stephenson gives us an erudite and reflective reconsideration of one of the twentieth century's most gifted poets, W. H. Auden, through an exploration of his WWII poem, *The Age of Anxiety*. The central but subtle use of Jung's views of the psyche, especially his typology, are shown to be woven through the poem, informing its deepest vision. This influence then ripples out through the musical and dance productions of the poem created by major artists. Internal and cultural worlds interpenetrate in this marvelous study that Stephenson deftly brings to life, not only in the post-World War 1940s and early 1950s, but in contemporary adaptations, thereby initiating us to Auden's prophetic gift. Stephenson's own creative brilliance manifests through the lightness of his touch.

—**Joe Cambray**, Ph.D., Provost and Vice President for Academic Affairs at Pacifica Graduate Institute. He is Past-President of the International Association for Analytical Psychology, former US Editor of the *Journal of Analytical Psychology*, and is the author of several books and numerous papers.

AGES OF ANXIETY

PUBLISHED BY:
SPRING JOURNAL, INC.
NEW ORLEANS, LOUISIANA, USA
WEBSITE: WWW.SPRINGJOURNALANDBOOKS.COM

COVER DESIGN:
ALEJANDRO MAGALLANES
MAGALLANES.GLZ@GMAIL.COM

Based in Mexico City, designer **Alejandro Magallanes** has built an international reputation for his posters, distinctive for their use of mixed media and visual impact. Alejandro works mainly for social and cultural media and has designed not only posters but books, animations, collages, letters, and images. He is a founding member of several activist poster groups whose work promotes peace, justice, and women's rights, and has written nine children's books and a recent collection of poems. Three monographs of his work as a graphic designer and poster designer have been published in China, Spain, and Germany.

TECHNICAL ASSISTANCE PROVIDED BY:
ERICA MATTINGLY
EEMATTINGLY@GMAIL.COM
NORTHERN GRAPHIC DESIGN & PUBLISHING
INFO@NCARTO.COM

TEXT PRINTED ON ACID-FREE PAPER

LIBRARY OF CONGRESS CATALOGING-IN-PUBLICATION DATA PENDING

AGES OF ANXIETY

Jung's Types as Inspiration for Poetry, Music, and Dance

Craig E. Stephenson

SPRING JOURNAL BOOKS

PUBLICATIONS IN JUNGIAN PSYCHOLOGY
www.springjournalandbooks.com

TABLE OF CONTENTS

TABLE OF CONTENTS... V

ACKNOWLEDGEMENTS vii

PERMISSIONS ix

LIST OF FIGURES xi

INTRODUCTION.. 1

CHAPTER ONE: AUDEN, WAR POET.. 7

CHAPTER TWO: AUDEN'S USE OF JUNG'S TYPOLOGY 41

CHAPTER THREE: CREATIVE EXTRAPOLATIONS 75

CHAPTER FOUR: CONCLUSIONS 103

APPENDIX: AN ARCHETYPAL MAPPING OF A SOLDIER'S
    POST-WAR ANXIETY IN GRIMM'S "BEARSKIN"............................ 127

INDEX 137

ACKNOWLEDGEMENTS

Thanks to Nancy Cater for the invitation to write. Thanks to Murray Stein and to Erhard Trittibach and the Zürich Lecture Series Programme Committee for courageously taking up the proposal to present the lectures with a performance of Bernstein's music. Thanks to concert pianist Victoria Harmandjieva for her brilliant collaborative participation in these lectures and to concert pianist Benedek Horváth for stepping courageously into the orchestral role of the second piano at the last minute. Thanks to the Jungian Psychoanalytical Association, New York, and the organizers of the Psychological Types Conference, April 2015, for providing a first venue and vessel for these ideas. Thanks to Cecile Tougas for correcting the Latin. Thanks to Jackie Flanagan for two weeks of hospitality and calm at Millican House, Calgary, to finish the draft. Thanks to Danielle Castronovo, New York Public Library, Performing Arts Division, Special Collections for assistance with the Jerome Robbins archives, and to Amanda Corp at the London Library for research assistance. Thanks to Lucie Pabel and Gottwalt Pankow for information about Auden and the Hamburg Ballet and for arriving by surprise to the Zürich lectures with our dog Lucy so that she could "assister au spectacle" (as the French say). Thanks to Liam Scarlett, Artist in Residence, Royal Ballet, for answering my questions in the midst of rehearsals at the Koch Theater, NYC and to Ashley Whitfield, Head of the Royal Ballet Press, for setting up the meeting during the Royal Ballet's 2015 American tour. Thanks to Alejandro Magallanes for the dynamic cover design. Thanks to Stacy Wirth for friendship and dog stories and for her insightful observation that the Nazis would have classified Bernstein's compositions steeped in jazz as "degenerate art." Thanks, again, to Laurel Boone who interrupted her retirement and music camp to edit the manuscript. Thanks to Erica Mattingly for copyediting and to Bob Gagliuso at Northern Graphic Design and Publishing for guidance through the production process. And finally, so much more than thanks to my partner Alberto Manguel for inspiration, for fortitude, and for our home.

PERMISSIONS

A special note of gratitude to Edward Mendelson, literary executor for the W. H. Auden estate, especially for permission to reproduce his transcription of the Swarthmore College chart. Thanks to Penguin Random House and Steven Salpeter at Curtis Brown Ltd. for permission to quote W. H. Auden. Thanks to Lorraine Goonan at The ImageWorks, Mike Markiewicz at ArenaPAL, Gabryel Smith at New York Philharmonic, George P. Lynes II, New York Public Library, Leslie Wong at Bridgeman Image Library, Nora Egloff at The Leonard Bernstein Office Inc., and Getty Images. A version of the appendix appeared first as "The Psychotherapeutic Mapping of a Soldier's Suffering: A Narrative Analysis of Grimm's 'Bearskin'" in the first issue of the Canadian journal, Journal for Military, Veteran and Family Health (JMVFH).

LIST OF FIGURES

CHAPTER ONE

Figure 1: Auden with his father and brothers on holiday during World War One, Rhayader, Wales. TopFoto/The ImageWorks.

Figure 2: Auden and Christopher Isherwood, departure for China, January 1938. The ImageWorks.

Figure 3: Auden amongst the ruins of Nuremberg, May 1945. TopFoto/ The ImageWorks.

CHAPTER TWO

Figure 1: W. H. Auden, photograph by Jerry Cooke, January 1, 1946. The LIFE Picture Collection, Getty Images.

Figure 2: Auden and Chester Kallman, PEN Conference, Venice, 1949. Bridgeman Images.

Figure 3: Auden and Rhoda Jaffe, Fire Island, photograph by James Stern, 1946. Bridgeman Images.

Figure 4: Auden's formatting design for The Age of Anxiety, Random House, 1947. Author's collection.

CHAPTER THREE

Figure 1: Auden and Leonard Bernstein, photograph by Ben Greenhaus. New York Philharmonic Archives.

Figure 2: Leonard Bernstein, birthday greeting and musical sketch to Serge Koussevitzky, July 26, 1944. Holograph. Courtesy of the Leonard Bernstein Office, Boosey and Hawkes, and the Library of Congress.

Figure 3: Age of Anxiety, Jerome Robbins, Tanaquil Le Clercq, Roy Tobias, and Todd Bolender, choreography by Jerome Robbins, New York City Ballet, photograph by George Platt Lynes, 1950. Estate of George Platt Lynes and the New York Public Library.

Figure 4: Age of Anxiety, Jerome Robbins, Tanaquil Le Clercq, Roy Tobias, and Todd Bolender, Melissa Hayden, Herbert Bliss, Shaun O'Brien, Dick Beard, choreography by Jerome Robbins, New York City Ballet, photograph by George Platt Lynes, 1950. Estate of George Platt Lynes and the New York Public Library.

Figure 5: Age of Anxiety, choreography by John Neumeier, Ballet West, Jane Wood as Rosetta, Robert Arbogast as Quant, Jeffrey Rogers as Malin, Kristopher Payne as Emble, photograph by Mikel Covey, 1990. Printed with permission of Boosey & Hawkes Collection/ArenaPAL.

Figure 6: Age of Anxiety, choreography by Liam Scarlett, Royal Ballet, Bennet Gartside as Quant, Steven McRae as Emble, Laura Morera as Rosetta, Tristan Dyer as Malin, The Royal Ballet at the Royal Opera House, London, UK, photograph by Bill Cooper, November 5, 2014. Royal Opera House/ArenaPAL.

Figure 7: Age of Anxiety, choreography by Liam Scarlett, Royal Ballet, Bennet Gartside as Quant, Steven McRae as Emble, Laura Morera as Rosetta, Tristan Dyer as Malin, Kevin Emerton as Bartender, The Royal Ballet at the Royal Opera House, London, UK, photograph by Bill Cooper, November 5, 2014. Royal Opera House/ArenaPAL.

CHAPTER FOUR

Figure 1: W. H. Auden, Chart for a Swarthmore College seminar on Romanticism, 1943. Holograph. Reproduced with permission of the Estate of W. H. Auden.

Figure 2: W. H. Auden, Chart for a Swarthmore College seminar on Romanticism, 1943. Transcription by Edward Mendelson. Reproduced with permission of Edward Mendelson.

CHAPTER FIVE

Figure 1: Berserkers, The Lewis Chessmen, courtesy of the British Museum, London.

Figure 2: Hans Jakob Christoffel von Grimmelshausen, Der erste Beernhäuter, illustrated by Marcus Behmer, Berlin, published by Otto von Olten, Brandus'sche Verlagsbuchhandlung, 1919.

Figure 3: "Bearskin" in Grimm's Household Tales, translated by Marian Edwardes, illustrated by Robert Anning Bell, New York, Dutton, 1912, p. 87. New York Public Library. Accessed at https://archive.org/details/grimmshouseholdt00grim.

INTRODUCTION

*T*he *Age of Anxiety*, W. H. Auden's last dramatic book-length poem, is marked by a curious history and fortune. At the time of its publication in 1947, critics deemed it Auden's only failure; in spite of the adverse criticism, the poem won that year's Pulitzer Prize. Immediately afterwards, Leonard Bernstein took it up as the inspiration for his second symphony, named after Auden's poem, in which a solo pianist as protagonist engages in an anguished dialectic with the orchestra; after its first performance, in Boston, the symphony was dismissed by some and applauded by others. In 1950, the year in which Bernstein conducted the symphony in New York for the first time, Jerome Robbins premiered a ballet choreographed on Bernstein's music; this work, too, divided critics and audiences. Later, two more choreographers accepted the challenge to transpose Auden's poem and Bernstein's music into movement: in 1979, John Neuemeier devised his own choreography to Bernstein's symphony for the Hamburg Ballet, and in 1990 he reworked the piece for the American dance company Ballet West. More recently, in 2014, Liam Scarlett premiered his own composition for the Royal Ballet at Covent Garden, London. A year earlier, in 2013, the writer Scott Stossel published an account of his anxiety disorder entitled *My Age of Anxiety*. Stossel personalizes the title that Auden coined to define an era, for a book that is both a sweeping history of anxiety as mental illness and a moving memoir of mental distress, erudite, public, and, at the same time, intimate. Stossel describes humankind's evolutionary history of anxiety as illustrative of his own suffering and at the same time positions his suffering meaningfully and movingly within the context of ever-changing theories and diagnostic languages and treatment models. Auden, Bernstein, Robbins, Neuemeier, Scarlett, and Stossel: their six "Ages of Anxiety" are the ones to which my title refers.

My exploration of this series of artistic works begins with Carl Gustav Jung, whose writings inspired Auden to structure the dramatic action and voices of his poem on the framework of *Psychological Types*. Auden was an avid reader and critic of psychoanalytic literature. Tracking his interpretations of Jung's observations allows us to evaluate how effectively he used them and also, since he was one of the most prolific and intelligent twentieth-century critics (his *Collected Works* includes six volumes of critical prose), to note his doubts or concerns about Jung's theorizing. What can Auden teach us about Jung? And to what extent did Bernstein understand the Jungian framework of Auden's poem that was the inspiration for his second symphony? Did any of the three choreographers look back from Bernstein via Auden to Jung's *Psychological Types* in their own creative processes?

I'm also interested in critical responses to these "Ages of Anxiety" from a historical perspective. I want to consider the historical and cultural contexts within which the poem and the symphony, the dances, and the memoir were created, and to map the cumulative responses up to this day as a way of assessing where we are now, culturally and psychologically. For example, in the sixties, when Jungian literary interpretations were more in vogue, critics such as Edgar Callan and Tom Sawyer completed the preliminary work of identifying Jungian shadows and animas in Auden's *Age of Anxiety* and interpreted the poem as an allegory. Unfortunately, these writers showed a tendency to limit themselves to these identifications, using Auden's works to legitimize Jungian concepts such as the individuation process. This approach turns the poem into an exemplar of Jungian theory, rather than allowing Jungian theory to enrich an understanding and appreciation of the poem. Such readings now feel somewhat hackneyed. But academics at that time did at least establish that Auden read Jung seriously and worked out his responses to Jung through his writing, both prose and poetry. In the last years of the twentieth century, critic John Fuller took up the gargantuan task of identifying and weighing with an open and critical mind the significance of almost every source of Auden's writings, including, of course, the Jungian sources.

Auden's life and art were very closely linked. Edward Mendelson, Auden's literary executor, wrote two summations, *Early Auden* and *Later Auden*, and introductions to the volumes of the *Collected Works* he edited. In these brilliant books and essays, Mendelson guides the reader through Auden's oeuvre, chronicling in parallel the life and the poems. He confesses that he has "a bone to pick" with Jung, and expresses a certain sense of relief when Auden appears to relinquish Jung's ideas.

The critic Alan Jacobs, who edited and introduced a new edition of *The Age of Anxiety*[1], regrets that Auden's Jungian-based poem may be dated and unreadable, an opinion echoed in much current critical writing, which also dismisses Jungian theorizing as once-fashionable, now-dangerous modernist myth-making. This elicits the question of how carefully the critics have read Jung's work, or whether they've researched how Jungian theories about type have advanced since Jung first published *Psychological Types* (in German in 1921, in English in 1923). Catherine Gunther Kodat writes that if she had to, she would

> analyze *The Age of Anxiety* as a symptom of a particular double-voiced kind, making clear the poem's effectiveness in advancing US ambitions for global cultural significance while also drawing out its critical engagements with the nation's problematic reigning assumptions regarding sociality, gender, class, ethnicity, and sexuality.[2]

It's symptomatic of the state of critical thinking today that an important academic such as Kodat doesn't look deeper and merely remarks in passing what she would do *if* she had to. Like the Jungian critics of the sixties, today's academics make use of artistic works only to bolster the tenets of monolingual critical theory.

In my reading of *The Age of Anxiety* and its re-interpreters, I would like to offer, not a Jungian interpretation that places these artistic works in the service of Jungian theory, but an opportunity to ask how reading Jung carefully can work in service of Auden, Bernstein, and the other artists. Auden warned us that analytical psychologists may not be much inclined to formulate an effective aesthetic evaluation of works such as the ones I'm considering. He writes,

> [P]sychology, concentrating on the symbols, ignores words ... [and the] treatment of symbols and facts ... fails to explain why of two works dealing with the same unconscious material, one is aesthetically good and the other bad; indeed, ... few psychoanalysts in their published works show any sign of knowing that aesthetic standards exist.[3]

Bearing his caveat in mind, I intend to ask not only the question, How does *The Age of Anxiety* work?, but also, Is it any good?; and why did Bernstein, Robbins, Neumeier, Scarlett, and Stossel all recognize elements in Auden's poem to which they wanted to pay homage by carrying them forward and transposing them into their own creations?

My final concern is this: in 1973, around the time of Auden's death, the editors of the American Psychiatric Association's *Diagnostic and Statistical Manual of Mental Disorders* (*DSM*) were creating the diagnostic category of Post-traumatic Stress Disorder (PTSD), categorized as an "Anxiety Disorder." Recently, in 2013, the editors of the newly revised *DSM* moved PTSD from an anxiety disorder to a newly formed category, "Trauma and Stressor-related Disorders." This change in classification is, in part, a response to a wave of suicides by North American soldiers (both American and Canadian) returning from active service in Iraq or Afghanistan. The subsequent debate about veterans' accessibility to medical assistance focuses, among other details, on issues about our understanding of the connections between anxiety, depression, and trauma disorders. Veterans recognize the stigma if their anxious suffering is diagnosed as PTSD, a social idiom of mental distress, and relegated to the realm of the "not real" as an "anxiety neurosis" or as "war hysteria." A diagnosis of "brain trauma," on the other hand, renders the suffering "real" because the cause is organic and neurologically measurable. Nowhere in this diagnostic debate is there a place to pose the question: Does this suffering have meaning?

From 1943 until 1945, during the time Auden was composing *The Age of Anxiety*, he was wrestling with questions about anxiety and meaning in connection with how war affects consciousness. Jung's *Psychological Types* provided him with a vocabulary to formulate that inquiry.

Notes

1. W. H. Auden, *The Age of Anxiety*, ed. Alan Jacobs (Princeton, NJ: Princeton University Press, 2011).

2. Catherine Gunther Kodat, "Performance Anxieties: The A-Literary Companions of American Literary Studies," in *A Companion to American Literary Studies*, ed. Caroline F. Levander and Robert Levine (Oxford: Blackwell, 2011), pp. 125–38.

3. W. H. Auden, "Psychology and Art Today," in *The Collected Works of W. H. Auden*, prose, vol. 1, ed. Edward Mendelson (Princeton, NJ: Princeton University Press, 1997), p. 98.

Figure 1: Auden with his father and brothers, Rhayader, Wales.

CHAPTER ONE

AUDEN, WAR POET

War formed W. H. Auden's identity. The god of war claimed a place in the constellation of Auden's psyche and in the constitution of his personality. Reviewing an anthology entitled *War and the Poet* in 1946, he names this god "Hateful Ares," a combination of "fear and defiance, i.e., fear of being afraid, that … seduces Aphrodite and destroys the children of men." And yet in this same review Auden also writes more prosaically,

> [W]henever man attempts to solve any kind of problem dialectically he is in a state of peace; whenever he attempts to solve it eristically he is in a state of war. A dialectical relation between two opponents means that each emphasizes one aspect of a truth or belief which both hold in common and that the aim of both is to arrive at an agreement. An eristic relation means that each is aiming not at the conversion but at the annihilation of the other. … In psychology, repression is eristic, sublimation dialectical.[1]

Deliberately working against the politically eristic nature of his times, Auden created dialectical relations in a number of different works: in the plays he wrote with Christopher Isherwood, in the opera libretti he wrote with Chester Kallman, and especially in the four book-length poems that he wrote during the years 1939–1945, when the world was at war. The early collaborations with Isherwood and the later ones with Kallman were "love-work," he said, and more erotically joyful than any sexual experience.[2] Writing the extended poems—*The Age of Anxiety* (1947) in particular—was solitary and arduous war-work.[3]

Auden often identified with and struggled against an inclination to diagnose society's ills and prescribe treatments for the body politic. Eventually, he learned to listen carefully to his "clinical mindedness" but not give it full rein in his verse, to take up scientific, medical, and psychoanalytical languages in his prose but not prescribe social correctives in his poetry. In his 1939 elegy for W. B. Yeats, Auden famously stripped the Irish poet of his public persona with the caustic phrase, "Poetry makes nothing happen," and in a prose essay he insisted that Yeats as poet (and by implication, he himself) should not be judged on an ability to solve the problems of the times: "art is a product of history," he said, "not a cause."[4]

Auden certainly did not absolve himself from social engagement, but after he moved from England to the United States in January 1939, he reformulated his persona. Leaving behind a public role as the most articulate of the young British leftist intellectuals, he adopted the voice of a responsible private poet. Nor did he recuse himself; he had to earn a living in America by reviewing, teaching, and lecturing. In his critical writing he voiced very public positions, because he felt it was easier to be monolingual in prose, whereas poetic truth was more complicated. Even after his poems were published, he continually revised them whenever he detected a whiff of inflated rhetoric or assonances that smoothed over falsehoods. Still, at the end of the elegy for Yeats, Auden once again crowns the dead Irish poet as laureate while devising for him a new mandate that will be embodied in "the guts" of his living readers: to "teach the free man how to praise." These last words of the elegy are emphatic: "teach," educate, lead out; "free man," the man who exercises choice; and "to praise," to acclaim, to approve, to assign value. The new social responsibility of the poet, according to Auden, is to show people how best to articulate in order to affirm.

"September 1, 1939" illustrates both Auden's care not to prescribe and his concern with language. The poem describes evil unleashed and a tentative flickering network of tiny affirming flames: Eros opposing Ares, Eris, and Thanatos. In 1945, in a fit of self-editorial ruthlessness, Auden suppressed the poem from his *Collected Poems* because he identified as a lie its most famous line, "We must love one another or die." In interviews, he also pointed to its faulty logic: "We're all going to die, whether we love one another or not."

Auden may have acquired his inclination to be clinically minded, to diagnose social malaise, predict its outcome, and prescribe a cure, partly from his father, George Augustus Auden. A doctor, George served for a time as the Chief Medical Officer for Schools and Professor of Public Health at Birmingham University. He had taken a first in Natural Science in Cambridge in the 1890s, and he was an expert in Greek, Latin, and several modern languages, including Danish and German, from which he translated works on antiquities and archaeology. Extremely well read, he was not at all interested in conventional distinctions between the sciences and the humanities. His son said,

> In my father's library scientific books stood side by side with works of poetry and fiction, and it never occurred to me to think of one as being less or more 'humane' than the other. ... My father's library not only taught me to read, but dictated my choice of reading. It was not the library of a literary man nor of a narrow specialist, but was a heterogeneous collection of books on many subjects, and included very few novels. In consequence, my reading has always been wide and casual rather than scholarly, and in the main non-literary.[5]

At one time, George worked as Honorary Psychologist to a children's hospital, and in his library Auden acquainted himself with W. H. R. Rivers' *Instinct and the Unconscious* (1920) and with the works of Freud. In his last year of secondary school, he told a friend, Michael Davidson, that he wanted to train as a psychologist.

George Auden garnered a reputation as the kind of doctor who cared more for his individual patients than for the special features of their diseases, an empathetic orientation that his son admired and sought to emulate.[6] In an early drama entitled *Paid on Both Sides: A Charade*, about a generation-old conflict between the Nowers and the Shaws, Auden inserts into the plot a stock figure from mummers' plays, named "Doctor." The protagonist John Nower has shot the antagonist Spy Shaw. The farcical doctor enters, farting while removing a bicycle pump, a circular saw, and other tools from his medical bag. Nonetheless, he speaks wisely when he observes, "The conscious brain appears normal except under emotion," and also when he diagnoses the problem: "Adamant will, cool brain, and laughing spirit." Thanks to the doctor's intervention (including extracting a tooth that has been growing for ninety-nine years, since before the great-grandmother's generation), the antagonist-victim recovers.

Now, for a time, the dialectic can resume.[7] In "The Art of Healing: In Memoriam David Protetch, M.D.," a poem Auden wrote much later in life in memory of his own general practitioner, he cites his father more explicitly: "'Healing,' / Papa would tell me, / 'is not science, / but the intuitive art / of wooing Nature.'"[8]

Auden was born in 1907, and his first experience of war was of his father's absence. George joined the Royal Army Medical Corps in August 1914, and, during four years, he served in Gallipoli, Egypt, and France. Auden's two older brothers had already been at boarding school, and shortly after his father's enlisting, Auden was sent away to school as well. The lease of the family house was terminated, and Auden's mother moved in with relatives. For a time, Auden had no settled home to which to return from school, and he did not see his father again until he was twelve. Very much later, he wrote about this rupture and its consequences. Although George had returned from the war, Auden felt that, at an age when he needed his father the most, he had been abandoned. For this reason, he and his father never fully connected.[9]

Auden's mother, Constance Rosalie Bicknell, compounded the difficulties caused by the absence of his father. When she was a young child, Constance had lost both her parents, and when she was eighteen, the unmarried uncle who had raised her died. She had a strong personality and was unusually independent-minded for a woman of her generation. Also unusual for the time, she had graduated (in French) with a gold medal from Royal Holloway College, London, before training as a nurse. She intended to serve as an Anglican medical missionary. Instead, she met and married Dr. George Auden, a man whose social status, she thought, was lower than her own. After giving birth to her first two sons, Bernard and John, she had a miscarriage. Wystan was her fourth pregnancy. She had no more children.

Auden's connection with his mother was strong but problematic. He associated her power with music, with her and his own piano playing. She taught him the love potion scene from Wagner's *Tristan and Isolde*, perhaps oblivious to the incestuous aspect of their singing it together. Auden also derived from her a passion for the rituals of High Mass in the Anglo-Catholic church, augmented by a combined family legacy of two grandfathers who had been vicars and died young. Reading his father's Freud at the age of 15, Auden recognized the tension between his very strong connection to his mother's imaginative life and his own solitude.

Auden wrestled for much of his adult life with the psychological implications of his mother's piety as well as with her conditional love. On the one hand, she loved him profoundly, as he did her; on the other hand, she disapproved of what she eventually discovered in her third and favorite son—his loss of faith, his homosexuality, his poor grades at Oxford, his leftist politics. Auden described the resulting dilemma for himself as a child in an unpublished ditty:

> Tommy did as mother told him
> Till his soul had split;
> One half thought of angels
> And the other half of shit.[10]

Auden was stuck in a "double bind," the term the anthropologist and philosopher Gregory Bateson coined in his *Steps to An Ecology of Mind*[11] to describe psychologically a child's experience of a mother who says "I love you" while turning her head away. This struggle would have been particularly difficult during the years when the counterpoint of his father's calm presence and gentle agnosticism was completely absent.

Auden understood this double bind very well. In 1942, he wrote to his friend James Stern with startling immediacy about the emotions he had once experienced: "You would be surprised how unpleasant too much parental love and interest can be, and what a torture of guilt it makes breaking away."[12] Earlier he had reflected, "Intellectual achievement, especially artistic, grows from the child's attempt to 'understand the mechanism of the trap' in which it finds itself."[13] Combining recollection and psychological reflection in his poem "Letter to Lord Byron" (1936), Auden encapsulated this insight into an aphorism concerning the usefulness of the psychological complex for creating both consciousness and character: "Let each child have that's in our care/ As much neurosis as the child can bear."[14]

George and Constance Auden, individually and through their marriage, provided a template of both unity and contrast, George standing for stability, common sense, and reality, and Constance for surprise, eccentricity, and fantasy.[15] The young Auden consciously identified himself with his father's agnosticism until eventually he professed himself an atheist, but his more non-rational religious attitude was never far off. Christopher Isherwood complained that, in their dramatic work, he had to prevent Auden's contributions from shifting from irony into magical rites. "When we collaborate," he said, "I have to keep a sharp eye on him—or down flop the characters on their knees. ... If Auden had his way, he would turn every play into a cross between grand opera and high mass."[16] Likewise, Auden professed to scorn Romanticism but revered the prophetic visions of William Blake and the epic imagination of Goethe.[17] He distanced himself from orthodox religion for much of his adult life, and yet he employed as touchstones his memories of two visionary experiences (which I will later describe), one of agape, one of eros, as numinous, life-altering epiphanies. And then, in response to World War II, he quietly, even surreptitiously, returned to the Church.

Between the ages of seven and eleven Auden lived in a country at war. It's not surprising, then, to find a report from 1917 of the Officers' Training Corps at St. Edmund's School, in which Auden, his brother John, and the other boys participated in field days and conducted military operations.[18] And in the summer of 1922, Auden voluntarily attended an annual camp of the Gresham school's Officer Training Corps, a decision friends considered strange, since he was the most unlikely of soldiers, being physically awkward and usually cynical of such things.[19]

As a child, Auden was fascinated by mining landscapes and machinery, and he wanted to become a mining engineer. The unlikely vocation of poet descended upon him one day when he was walking with Robert Medley, a school friend upon whom he had developed a crush and who later recorded the incident. Medley asked him in passing if he wrote poetry. Only then did it occur to Auden that one could, and the question seemed to spark a realization more than it inspired a reflection. Medley appears to have functioned more as a catalyst than as a muse to a psychological fact of personality *in potentia*.[20]

Constellating this poetic vocation provoked some inner conflict but was too strong to be dismissed. Another school friend, John Pudney, recalled that, in 1925, Auden showed him manuscripts of some poems, but later, as they passed the school ponds, Auden flung the pages into the water. Pudney wrote that Auden declared "he had got poetry out of his system once and for all and that the human race would be saved by science."[21] That evening, Auden summoned friends to keep watch while he waded back into the pool to try to retrieve the pages.

Although Auden went up to Christ Church, Oxford, in 1925 to study Natural Sciences, in 1926 he switched to reading Philosophy, Politics, and Economics. By the autumn of 1926, he had changed his field to English, which at the time was not considered a serious academic subject. At Oxford, it was next to impossible to find a professor willing to supervise such a course of study.

In his reflective 1942 letter to James Stern about his upbringing, Auden described the persistent mixed feelings stirred up after his father's return from the war. These feelings sparked even a sexual longing: "When I was 15, I was on a walking tour with my father, and we were sharing a bed: I suddenly had a most violent longing to be fucked by him. (Not being a novelist, I have to confess that he didn't.)"[22] An orthodox Freudian might say that Auden was dangerously over-identified with his mother's psychology (an interpretation with which Auden would have sometimes agreed), but I think most Freudians now would read the Oedipal conflict with more subtlety. The anecdote expresses explicitly the desire to summon the absent father into his presence, to be penetrated by his father, to be possessed sexually by the father, in other words, to be initiated by the father into sexuality and adulthood. In the summer of 1925, Auden traveled with his father to Austria, and they went to Yugoslavia in 1927. These were difficult trips. Did Auden feel that they were too late to address his need to know and be known by his father? Traveling together revealed their differences—different temperaments, different inclinations, different choices—which must have been hard for both father and son to endure, with that raw longing to connect so palpable and strong. Just the same, a few days after his return from Yugoslavia, Auden wrote what Mendelson identifies as the first piece in which the young poet discovered his own voice. This pivotal poem of thirty lines entitled "The Watershed" describes a highly charged readiness: "Ears pose before decision, scenting danger."[23]

In 1928, after receiving a humiliating third-class degree in his final examinations at Oxford, Auden went to Spa, Belgium, for three weeks. Here, for the first and only time, he tried psychoanalysis. To his brother John, he wrote about the experience: "I wish to improve my inferiority complex and to develop heterosexual traits." To his friend Isherwood, he wrote with a different tone: "Had a most pleasant week with my analyst. Libido, it is proved is towards women. The trouble is incest."[24] In a note to another friend, David Ayerst, he wrote more optimistically, "I find I am quite ambidextrous now," which seems to suggest that he may have experimented sexually or at least allowed himself to fantasize about bisexuality.[25] Certainly, in three weeks, little more could have been accomplished than defining the presenting problem. Even that would have required the careful differentiating of a number of intertwined threads, including Constance's piety and willfulness and Auden's own atheism, his homosexuality, his poor showing at Oxford, his aloneness, and his highly charged poetic vocation. He had told his Oxford tutor Nevill Coghill that he was going to be, not just a poet, but a "great" one, and yet he still felt that a literary vocation was inferior to a scientific one, because science changes the world. All told, in 1928, the "analysis" lasted only three weeks, and little is known about the psychoanalyst with whom he consulted.[26]

After Auden returned from Belgium, his father provided him with an allowance for an exploratory year off before having to look for work. Most English artists at the time were strongly Francophile, and their *porte d'entrée* into all things aesthetic was Paris. Auden chose Germany, even though he would have to learn the language, and even though (or perhaps partly because) his mother Constance had distinguished herself in French. In October 1928 he went to Berlin for the year, isolating himself from family and friends and also from his early poetic influences. He kept journals on his reading of Freud and his careful exploration and examination of his erotic life and sexuality. For example, he noted how much more exciting eros was before it was physically consummated, and he recorded how guilt about his homosexuality continued to torment him as a wound or a weakness.[27]

As well as studying Freud, Auden read D. H. Lawrence's literary counter-criticism of psychoanalysis in *Fantasia of the Unconscious*.[28] He also learned from his new Berlin friend, John Layard, about the American educator and psychologist Homer Lane, who had treated Layard psychotherapeutically for paralysis. Lane, who had no professional training, posited a psychological redefinition of criminality and morality in terms of repressed instinct. Layard edited Lane's only published work, a collection of lectures called *Homer Lane Talks to Parents and Teachers* (1928). Compared to Freud's mapping of individual neuroses, Lane's social experiments (for example, his "Little Commonwealth," a co-educational community for "delinquents" created in Dorset, England) felt radical, an edgy mixture of Rousseau and Nietzsche. From Layard[29], Auden also learned about Georg Groddeck, the German pioneer of psychosomatic medicine, whose work provided Freud with the designation of the "Id/It."[30] Lawrence, Lane, and Groddeck all posited psychodynamic arguments about somatic disease and mental disorder as symptoms of conflict between the conscious and the unconscious mind, a war in which not only individual sufferers but also entire cultural groups and nations were implicated.

In the 1928 elections, the Nazi party won only 2.5% of the German vote, but both the communists and the brownshirts were visible in the streets of Berlin. Auden remembered the Nazis in those days as forlorn, shabby beggars[31], but he could see in them a German nationalism tainted with something archaic and dangerous. "The Nazis have a theory that Iceland is the cradle of Germanic culture," he said in a letter. "Well, if they want a community like that of the sagas they are welcome to it. I love the sagas, but what a rotten society they describe, a society with only the gangster virtues."[32] Auden witnessed the Weimar Republic's progressive disarray. His poem "1929" begins with strolling at Easter in the public gardens, the clouds "moving without anxiety on open sky," and moves in the second section to "anxiety at night," his own concealed anger amid the shootings and barricades of the May Day conflict between the communists and the police that left 23 dead.[33] Looking back, Auden identified these days as the first time he felt politically aware, but in Germany he was a disengaged outsider, a "stranger to strangers," as he put it in "The Wanderer."[34] At the end of his year away, he returned to England with his outsider's perspective intact—"as the hawk sees it or the helmeted airman"—but ready to give voice, as he could not in Germany, to a prophetic fury at his own country's social and moral malaise: "Seekers after happiness, all who follow / The convolutions of our simple wish, / It is later than you think."[35]

After the bohemian lifestyle and frightening politics of Berlin, Auden chose the opposite extreme, teaching in English private schools, from 1930 to 1935. He enjoyed teaching, and he needed to earn a living. On the side, he wrote book reviews in which he honed his critical expertise. For instance, in "Poetry, Poets, and Taste," he defended the arts against he-men, doctors, and social reformers, against the English patriarchal suspicion of expressiveness and the scientific dismissal of art as neurotic social evasiveness. Reiterating the importance of seeing "as the hawk sees it," Auden writes, "The artist is the person who stands outside and looks, stands even outside himself and looks at his daydreams." As much as they may need to make money and want to amuse friends, he argues, artists tell truths which others are too busy or too ashamed to see, in order to strengthen the individual and collective will. In closing, Auden makes an important aesthetic statement: "Personally the kind of poetry I should like to write but can't is the thoughts of a wise man in the speech of the common people."[36]

The poems Auden wrote at this time evoke a private life and love precariously juxtaposed against personal and national foreboding. In "A Summer Night," written in 1935, he describes a quiet shared epiphany of connection and freedom between friends sitting together out on a lawn and sets it against images of flooding, of "sudden death before our eyes."[37] The speaker asks hard questions that he and his friends have been too content or too ashamed to ask: "What doubtful act allows our freedom in this English house, our picnics in the sun?" This speaker, lying out at night and looking at his feet, at first self-reflecting, now looks up and follows the moon's impartial trajectory and gains a double perspective: a memory of the intimate connection between friends on the lawn and an image of that contentment as walled in, with the dykes about to crumble, rent by floodwaters.

Auden considered the incident behind "A Summer Night" one of the most important in his life. Nearly thirty years later, he reported what had happened. One night in 1933, he and three other teachers sat outdoors chatting about unimportant things. All at once, Auden felt himself overcome by a feeling of love, not romantic, familial, or sexual, but general, the kind of love for other people known as agape. This joy in shared humanity overwhelmed his shame over how disagreeable he had been in the past, and he felt that he should never hurt anyone again. The feeling was diminished by morning, and after a few days, he returned to his normal, more careless treatment of others. Even so, he verified with one of the other teachers that he had not been alone in the experience, and that, he said, "made it much more difficult for me to deceive myself about what I am up to when I do [treat others badly]." This experience, turned to poetry in "A Summer Night," helps explain why, in his essay "Poetry, Poets, and Taste," he would want not just to articulate the approaching menace but to offer something "wise" in response.

In the summer of 1935 Auden gave up school teaching. He also married Erika Mann, an actress and the daughter of Thomas Mann, so that she could become a British subject after Goebbels took away her German citizenship. (Although they never had a marital relationship, they never divorced, either.)[38] In January 1936 he decided to take part in the civil war in Spain. In a letter to E. R. Dodds, he explained why: "I so dislike everyday political activities that I won't do them, but here is something I can do as a citizen and not as a writer, and as I have no dependents, I feel I ought to go." Then, a few days later, he wrote to Dodds a second time with a different explanation for his decision: as a poet, he had to learn everything he possibly could about the human condition; otherwise, how could he speak to—or for—humanity? The only way he could achieve such knowledge was to get personally involved.[39] These two letters present different reasons for going to Spain—one addresses the public act of the citizen, while the other speaks of the private intentions of the poet. Mendelson interprets Auden's inability to give voice to both reasons in the same letter to the same friend as evidence of an important inner conflict or psychological splitting.

Auden intended to volunteer as an ambulance driver with the Spanish Medical Aid Committee, but instead he was put to work in propaganda broadcasting in support of the Republic. In March, after only three months in Barcelona and Valencia, he quietly returned to England. He spoke little about his experiences. Only much later, in an essay written in 1955, did he mention, for instance, how shocked and disturbed he felt when he discovered the Republic's brutality and the anti-clerical Communists' burning of the churches in Barcelona.

In May 1937, Auden published the pamphlet poem, *Spain*, with the proceeds going to Medical Aid for Spain. In an essay entitled "Inside the Whale," George Orwell both praised the poem as "one of the few decent things that have been written about the Spanish war" and, at the same time, famously took Auden to task for employing the phrase "necessary murder," which he attacked as rhetoric akin to Stalinist words like "liquidation" and "elimination." Orwell acknowledged having already spitefully described Auden as a "gutless Kipling" for early poems that, on the surface, appeared ironic or parodic but that, deeper down, resounded with boy-scout "uplift." Now Orwell identified in Auden's *Spain* an amoralism "that was only possible for those who are personally immune," who are always "somewhere else when the trigger is pulled."[40] Orwell's attack stung, but Auden eventually rejected his own poem on similar grounds. He judged that the concluding phrase of the poem—"History to the defeated / May say Alas but cannot help or pardon"—was a lie. Elsewhere he called this equating of virtue and success a "wicked doctrine" and reproached himself for writing it "simply because it sounded to me rhetorically effective."[41] Orwell's criticism seems to have pricked Auden's conscience and consciousness about his two reasons for having decided to go to the war in Spain. To what extent was he, as citizen, still "personally immune" to (that is, not yet changed/infected/ altered by) the war to which he bore witness? And to what degree did his lofty hawk's-eye perspective render his poetry susceptible to intellectual abstraction and rhetorical inauthenticity?

That same year, Auden and Isherwood received a commission to write a travel book about Asia, and when Japan invaded China, they decided to travel to China to witness first-hand the invasion by the Japanese Imperial Army. They sailed from England to Hong Kong, and in February 1938 they entered China by way of Canton, visiting Hankow, Sian, and the front lines at Sü-chow and Mei-ki. The book they published, *Journey to a War* (1939), consisted of a prose narrative written by Isherwood based on their travel diaries, and poetry and photographs by Auden.

An opening sonnet, dedicated to E. M. Forster, sets the tone for the book as a whole. In it, Auden asks if art, like a telephone, can interrupt and wake us from our political single-mindedness with the possibility of dialectic.[42] Fascism promotes unity at the cost of freedom and the inner life, he says, and he gratefully depicts Forster's stories as stones that trip us up as we run gladly, *en masse*, down the fascist slope of Hate. At the end of the poem, the figure of Miss Avery (from Forster's novel *Howard's End*) comes out into the garden holding aloft a sword. In the novel, this is Margaret Schlegal's father's sword, unsheathed, and Miss Avery, carrying the sword, speaks the truth: that the death of Leonard Bast is "murder." She is also like the angel who blocks Adam and Eve from slipping back into any enchanted state of Eden-like ignorance.[43]

Journey to a War is a remarkable book. In particular, a sequence of twenty-seven sonnets entitled "In Time of War" is the culmination of Auden's work in the 1930s.[44] An intimate and ferociously honest exercise in collective memory and conscience, the poems trace human history from Eden to the present in order to disenchant. Mendelson argues that Auden achieved his goal in part by reversing forms, by taking up the intimate sonnet form that he had reserved mostly for love poems in a private voice and employing it to frame his larger public

Figure 2: Auden and Christopher Isherwood, departure for China, January 1, 1938.

themes. Each individual sonnet accumulates small intense particulars, and the discipline of fourteen rhymed lines pre-empts any possibility of bombast or bloated pronouncements:

> Here war is simple like a monument:
> A telephone is speaking to a man;
> Flags on a map assert that troops were sent;
> A boy brings milk in bowls. There is a plan

For living men in terror of their lives,
Who thirst at nine who were to thirst at noon,
And can be lost and are, and miss their wives,
And, unlike an idea, can die too soon.

But ideas can be true although men die,
And we can watch a thousand faces
Made active by one lie:

And maps can really point to places
Where life is evil now:
Nanking; Dachau.[45]

The twenty-seven sonnets, one after the other, accumulate density and heft. As a whole, they also acquire the momentum or positive inertia of a narrative and a literary argument. They function as the equivalent to W. H. R. Rivers' anthropological treatise about the human capacity for violence,[46] except that Auden came to value his sonnet sequence not as an argument but as a string of parables.

Later Auden wrote an afterword to the sonnet sequence, a poetic "Commentary" that was also a conclusion to the book. Even though the sonnets conveyed a shift in technique and even a new poetic stance, Mendelson characterizes the addendum of the "Commentary" as regressive, a stepping backwards, and Auden himself felt doubtful about the tone of this concluding piece. Here again were the hawk-like perspective, the didacticism, and the rhetorical posturing that had undermined poems such as "Spain." Auden knew that his praise for the civil reconciliation of Chinese Communists and Nationalists against the Japanese was politically motivated and misrepresented what he and Isherwood had witnessed. On the one hand, was it aesthetically astute to give the "Commentary" the last word in the book if it undermined the artistic effect of the whole?[47] On the other hand, how could one invoke the political principle of an inclusive dialectic and then deliberately—murderously—edit out of the literary text the insistent values of the leftist intellectual, to say nothing of the platitudes of the English vicar?

The aesthetic problem presented by the "Commentary" to *Journey to a War* also crystallized as a personal dilemma when Auden returned to England. Travel had changed him, bearing witness to the Sino-Japanese war had changed him, and he was personally less "immune" (to use Orwell's word). But he found himself caving in to social pressures, falling back into the old familiar role of the pontificator or, more precisely, what Mendelson calls the "Court Poet of the Left" by lecturing, for instance, on the anti-fascist struggle in China. Around this time, too, Auden occasionally employed the image of smothering family confinement in order to define his professional predicament: "I felt the situation for me in England was becoming impossible. I couldn't grow up. English life is for me a family life, and I love my family but I don't want to live with them."[48] At the same time, he wrote a parable entitled "The Sportsmen" (1938) in which English artists are represented as duck-hunters who, because of various socio-economic and ecological decisions and class distinctions in the village, no longer find genuine "ducks" to hunt. Therefore they decide to produce clay-and-paper decoys; the young, not knowing the difference, admire the artist-hunters for their skill, while the old know that they are lying.[49] Finally, in a 1939 essay, "Democracy's Reply to the Challenge of Dictators," Auden as a former schoolteacher described his dilemma in terms of the education system in England:

> I think teachers are going to be much more interested in adult education and less in child education, because democracy does not imagine that people are finished when they are 14, 18, 21, or whatever age we turn them out, and that after that they having nothing to do but to carry out their jobs. Naturally the Fascist States are extremely interested in child education, because they do not want people to develop on their own. To them, if the child can receive its ideas by the time it is 12, then the chief work is done, apart from vocational training. In a Fascist State the only general education required of the average citizen is military. But in a Social Democracy education has a double task: to train for a particular vocation, and to equip all citizens for an intelligent political life. *Frankly I am not very optimistic about what the bulk of teachers in this country are likely to do.*[50] (italics mine)

Taking his own temperature and not feeling sanguine about his prognosis, Auden decided he had to leave England. Miss Avery had indeed unsheathed the sword like the angel at the portal of Eden, forcing Auden to call nostalgia a death wish. To choose life, he had to choose loss, an expulsion. Not simply to travel, but to depart and not come back.

In an interview in 1965, Auden claimed that his decision to leave England had already been made as early as 1936. "I knew then that if I stayed," he said, "I would inevitably become a member of the British establishment."[51] But it was perhaps not until he and Isherwood had passed through Vancouver and traveled across North America to New York City on their journey from China back to Europe that Auden knew where he could go.

Auden and Isherwood left by ship from Southampton. They arrived in New York on January 26, 1939 and became "resident aliens," foreigners permitted to stay in the country permanently. That same day, Barcelona fell to Franco. Two days later, on January 28, Yeats died. As already mentioned, Auden's first poem written in the US, the elegy to Yeats, strips both the Irish poet and himself of any heroic function. At the same time, it seeks redress in an affirmative poetic mandate expressed in koan-like paradoxes: to "make a vineyard of the curse"; to "sing of human unsuccess / in a rapture of distress"; and "in the prison of his days, / [to] teach the free man how to praise."[52]

Auden began to experience his own divided self with increasing dismay. On March 16, 1939, he spoke the following words at the Foreign Correspondents' Dinner Forum, an event held to raise money for refugees from the Spanish war:

> If we interpret brotherhood as meaning we must do nothing to hurt anybody's feelings, if we use our liberty of speech not to find out how best to do things, but to air our learning and show off our personalities … then it will not be long before we suffer a worse fate than that of Spain, worse because it will not be tragic. For it will not be Germany, it will not be Italy, but our own people who will say 'To hell with talk, to hell with truth, to hell with freedom,' will rise up and sweep us away, and by God, ladies and gentlemen, we shall deserve it.[53]

The event was a success, but the effect of his own words on his conscience was negative. Auden resolved that he could no longer trust his own motivation in performing the role of poet speaking about war at political functions. After this dinner, he wrote in two different letters to A. E. Dodds: "I suddenly found I could really do it, that I could make a fighting, demagogic speech and have the audience roaring. I felt just covered with dirt afterwards." In the second, "Never, *never* again will I speak at a political meeting."[54] Questioning what poetry could do in wartime, Auden also experienced the problem within himself as a conflict with his own moral judgment and his personal authenticity. In an early letter to Stephen Spender, he had spoken of "the false emotions, inflated rhetoric, empty sonorities" to which he was susceptible. He now re-imagined the problem: how to reconcile political integrity with "my own devil of inauthenticity?"[55]

On September 1, 1939, Germany invaded Poland. Two days later, Britain and France reluctantly declared war. Auden recalled that he opened at random the published diaries of Vaslav Nijinsky and read, "I want to cry but God orders me to go on writing. He does not want me to be idle."[56] In letters to E. R. Dodds, Auden described how he wrote the subsequent poem, "September 1, 1939." Nijinsky not only provided God's goad not to be idle, he also defined the crux of the matter, expressed in terms of his personal conflict with his possessive and powerful lover-impresario Diaghilev: "Some politicians are hypocrites like Diaghilev, who does not want universal love, but to be loved alone."[57] Auden transposes this: "For the error bred in the bone / Of each woman and each man / Craves what it cannot have, / Not universal love / But to be loved alone." Looking through the mad dancer's insight as through a lens,[58] Auden developed a new vision consisting of three parts: a developmental psychoanalytic assessment of Hitler's formative years; the broader social perspective of a historical examination of German nationalism, "the whole offence / from Luther until now / That has driven a culture mad"; and a Christian moral insight into the dynamics of evil—"Those to whom evil is done / Do evil in return." Still identifying with Nijinsky's fragile insights, Auden concludes: "All I have is a voice / To undo the folded lie."

And yet Auden came to reject this poem, first (as I mentioned earlier) one line, "we must love one another or die" for its logic, and eventually, the whole piece, for lying.[59] In spite of Auden's unequivocal rejection, critics still work very hard to resuscitate and reclaim it. In the same way, they reread his elegy for Yeats and counter the decisive statement, "Poetry makes nothing happen," by emphasizing the subsequent line and the completion of the thought: "it [poetry] survives, / a way of happening, a mouth." After the terrorist attacks of September 11, 2001, traumatized New Yorkers rediscovered and fervently quoted "September 1, 1939." Contradicting its author's assessment but attesting to his understanding of how poetry works, the poem now possesses a life of its own in the "guts" of its living readers, even if it cannot be found in his *Collected Poems*.

At the time, however, Auden remained adamant. In November 1939, he went to the Yorkville district of Manhattan to view the Nazi propaganda film *Sieg im Westen* that celebrated the conquest of Poland. He was shocked by the largely German-speaking audience's open hatred of the Poles. Biographer Richard Davenport-Hines wrote, "When Poles appeared on the screen he was startled to hear a number of people in the audience scream, 'Kill them!' ... 'I wondered then, why I reacted as I did against this denial of every humanistic value.'"[60] Davenport-Hines describes how this show of hatred in the cinema made Auden distrust "September 1, 1939" and suppress the entire draft of a new book, *The Prolific and the Devourer*. He realized that his faith in the liberal notion of human progress was no longer tenable.[61] The moment in the cinema was like an acid-bath; it stripped him of superfluities, down to the core of his dilemma as a poet whom God would not permit to be idle during wartime, but who no longer knew what to say. Perhaps not coincidentally, around this time Auden returned to the Church, to witness and participate in the sense of sin and hope enacted in its rituals.

People in England had started accusing Auden (and Isherwood) of desertion during wartime, an accusation that further increased Auden's doubts.[62] If he felt guilty about the timing of his departure, he decided not to express remorse. As a homosexual, would he have been permitted to serve directly? If so, would he have been co-opted, to his chagrin, to write propaganda, as he had been in Spain? At this time, because of wartime regulations, his royalties from British publishers stayed within the country, and he directed them to war relief. Even though he wished he could shed his old skin as Court Poet of the Left and burn it, he considered his move to New York voluntary exile rather than desertion, but, like Dante, his favorite poet, he forged his compositions after January 1939 not so much from a vertical hawk-height as from the horizontal perspective of an exile. Beginning with "September 1, 1939," this new perspective progressed through the four long American poems of war-work, the last of which is *The Age of Anxiety*, set on All Souls' Night, 1944 and published in 1947.

In the first of the four long war poems, "New Year Letter," Auden addresses his friend, Elizabeth Mayer, another resident alien. Ostensibly he speaks to her from Brooklyn as he watches the New Year's Eve festivities across the East River in Manhattan fade into the dawn of New Year's Day, 1940. During this solitary midnight vigil, Auden visits again the problem that "poetry makes nothing happen," or as he voices it this time, "No words men write can stop the war."[63] Auden considers the problem from many angles. For example, he differentiates between art and life, and asks how an *ars poetica* functions differently from a philosophy of how to live a good—that is, moral—life: "Art in intention is mimesis / But, realized, the resemblance ceases; / Art is not life and cannot be / A midwife to society, / For art is a *fait accompli*."[64] Likewise, he understands psychologically that he would do better not to attempt to edit his personality as he would a poem intended for publication. Order may be the goal of both life and art, but in life ordering cannot be willed, whereas art can reach a state of edited, polished completion. Instead, Auden cites the open-ended ordering life-goal of Gestalt: to incorporate consciously more and different selves into a complex dialectical process in which "each great I / Is but a process in a process / within a field that never closes."[65]

Auden also carefully differentiates between outer and inner life. At the cusp of a New Year in New York, he charts an inner realm of memories of old York in England, where he was born. He contrasts England, virtuous in its history, with the outer realm of New York, his chosen other world, the fully alienated land of liberty peopled by isolated lonely individuals, each in search of identity.[66] Auden understood that the English have known who they are hierarchically for a very long time. For instance, Auden's mother considered that, even though Auden's grandfathers were both vicars, the fact was well established that her people were her husband's betters. Within this English social structure, the only individuals who question identity are either "foreigners" or "bounders," people with suspicious motives who seek to leap over established boundaries of class. Auden acknowledges that he must now learn to navigate within an utterly established and conservative inner psychic landscape and also in an outer life grounded in the essential aloneness that is the correlative of liberty and the pursuit of happiness.

In "New Year Letter," Auden acknowledges the literary cosmologies mapped by his favorite writers: Inferno, Purgatorio, and Paradiso in Dante's *Divine Comedy*; Heaven, Hell, and the Just City in Blake's *Jerusalem*; and the Romantic "smashing of the given" and "descent into the Other" in Rimbaud's *Une saison en enfer*. Auden also refers to other writers whose perspectives shaped his formulations: Baudelaire, Hardy, Kipling, and Rilke. Outside literature, Auden cites Marx on the rise of fascism and the impotence of democracy. He also cites Freud to understand Marx's distrust of privilege in society: that people who are ashamed of failure compulsively deny their self-doubt. But these were familiar citations from his work of the 1930s. Now Auden introduces religion into his poetic equation, in order to render personal his inner conflict as poet and citizen in wartime. Auden describes a figure both external and internal: the "diabolical schismatic," the "Prince of Lies," but, more personally, his own devil of inauthenticity. Ironically, this negative Daimon is particularly adept at misquoting Auden's favorite authors back at him in order to undermine his convictions.[67] In fact, the Devil proves to be a rather complicated fellow, responsible for introducing into Creation and into the act of creating the curse of disunity. With the curse come the gifts of double vision and dialectic. He is, then, the father of lies but also of poetry: he is "Legion,"[68] "the many" that contains and is contained by "the One." This personification helps Auden understand why feelings of inauthenticity accompany his feelings of inspiration.[69]

Here, Mendelson's critical astuteness is especially useful, because he classifies "New Year Letter" as structurally an epic poem. Auden usually began to compose by choosing a form, and in this case he modeled "New Year Letter" on Alexander Pope's *Essay on Man* (1734), the quintessential philosophical poem of the English Enlightenment, composed in heroic couplets. But Mendelson argues that "New Year Letter" is also aligned with Goethe's *Faust*. Epic poems call into question the social orders within which they are embedded—*Faust* begins in the cosmology of German classical aesthetics, which falls away by the end of Part II. And of course, in Goethe's masterwork, Mephistopheles drives the narrative and the literary argument forward. Auden regarded the dramatic structure of *Faust* as a failure. He saw it as a treasury of poetry and aphorism, but he found it episodic, one scene after another, without continuity. The same might be observed about "New Year Letter." And yet, what changes in our reading if we consider the poem, following Mendelson's suggestion, as an epic?[70]

At the beginning of "New Year Letter," Auden writes, "Though language may be useless, for / No words men write can stop the war," and then he completes his thought, "Yet truth, like love and sleep, resents / Approaches that are too intense."[71] Auden describes his dilemma: in war-time, how to use language not to propagandize but to engage with truth, personified as the Oracle, knowing that the psychopompos, the guider of souls, no longer answers direct questions. By the end of the epic, once all the historical anecdotes and literary citations have fallen away, "New Year Letter" communicates neither the force of a direct political argument nor the vision of a new social proposition, only the humble prayer to learn "To what conditions we must bow / In building the Just City now."[72] Epistemologically, Auden is convinced that the kind of truth needed will emerge only indirectly, in words and images that address not the middle-aged poet's questions but the "child of his distress."[73] Auden planned to publish this monologue, thereby rendering it public and available "to all / Who wish to read it anywhere." Even so, he cast it as a "private minute" addressed and dedicated to his much admired friend Elizabeth Mayer in an attempt to protect the tone from shifting back to bombast or despair. If in wartime, and in an epic structure, the epistemological framework upon which the century hangs falls away, then, how to speak? In "New Year Letter," the tentative answer is to speak with humility, to invoke indirectly the possibility of poetic truth. And speak in order to connect, as in E. M. Forster's famous admonition, and as Auden's poem affirms.[74]

After the first-person monologue of "New Year Letter," the three longer works that followed were all verse dramas about conflicts among people.[75] *For the Time Being* (1940–1942) is subtitled "A Christmas Oratorio," and Auden worked here with a diverse range of liturgical forms, including the miracle play and the nativity play.[76] The literary argument is in no way rational because by now Auden is convinced that reason is ineffectual. In his lifetime, reason and humanism had not led to peace and prosperity; they couldn't even prevent another war.[77] Indeed, one of Auden's jokes in *For the Time Being* is to cast King Herod, the traditional Christmas villain and murderer of the innocents, as a liberal humanist.[78]

The Sea and the Mirror (August 1942–February 1944) is a commentary on Shakespeare's *Tempest*, delivered as a series of dramatic monologues by characters from the play. In a transcribed conversation, Auden said that Shakespeare left *The Tempest* in a mess, but the mess itself was a kind of achievement that acknowledged the limits of form, something Auden warmly endorsed and wanted to explore.[79] By 1942 Auden was finding that not only reason but also form was becoming obsolete. The difficult discoveries were waiting to be found in opposing oneself, in the drama between the warring aspects of the creative imagination, in the mess. For instance, rather like his joke of making King Herod an articulate liberal humanist, Auden gives Caliban the most sophisticated voice he knew, that of Henry James, to great effect. This is not simply ironic; Auden also renders the voice Neo-Calvinist because Caliban's grotesque abasement, his assumption of always being in the wrong, is, according to Auden, the ethical position of believers.[80] This position is best articulated by Kierkegaard, whom Auden was reading at the time. Auden eventually argues even more directly in a later poem, "The Cave of Making," that the greatest disenchantment of the war lay in the loss of faith in one's own moral judgment, the recognition that "we shan't, not since Hitler and Stalin, / trust ourselves ever again: we know that, subjectively, / all is possible."[81]

In "W. H. Auden Speaks of Poetry and Total War," an article published in March 1942 in *The Chicago Sun*, Auden had stripped the arts of any exaggerated importance left over from the now suspect legacy of Romanticism, any notion of artists as "the unacknowledged legislators of the world" or, conversely, as the makers of art for art's sake who have no

Figure 3: Auden amongst the ruins of Nuremberg, May 1945.

responsibility to society. In a time of war, Auden was particularly wary of poets' colluding with aestheticizing violence and shrill patriotism. He counters his own "devil of inauthenticity" by invoking the counter-voice of World War I soldier-poet Wilfred Owen:

> If the poet, qua poet, has any other social function than to give pleasure, it is, in the words of the greatest poet produced by the last war, 'to warn,' so that, in one sense, the serious poetry of any given moment is always at odds with the conscious ideas of the majority.[82]

The social function of the poet in the extremes of wartime is compensatory.

In 1944, Auden started work on *The Age of Anxiety*, but an opportunity to serve the United States War Department interrupted his writing. From May until August 1945, he interviewed German civilians for the Morale Division of the United States Strategic Bombing Survey.

Auden, his friend James Stern, and a number of other German-speaking civilians were given military uniform and rank (Auden became a U.S. Army major) and traveled to German cities including Kempten, Erlangen, and Munich. Ostensibly, the purpose of the interviews was to discover the effect of Allied bombings on civilian "morale." Auden valued the opportunity to contribute actively but remained extremely skeptical about the work itself:

> This Morale title is illiterate and absurd. How can one learn anything about morals, when one's actions are beyond any kind of morality? Morale with an 'e' at the end is psycho-sociological nonsense. What they want to say, but don't say, is how many people we killed and how many buildings we destroyed by that wicked bombing.[83]

The procedure was for each member of the team to meet alone in a room with a German civilian who had been selected at random and to ask questions. "We asked them if they minded being bombed. We went to a city which lay in ruins and asked if it had been hit. We got no answers that we didn't expect."[84] Auden retold how, in Darmstadt, he was billeted at the home of a Nazi couple who had gone into hiding, leaving their children with the grandparents. "When the couple came home, I was the one who had to tell them that the grandparents had killed themselves—and had taken it upon themselves to kill their grandchildren, too."[85] At the same time, traveling within Germany permitted Auden to make inquiries about the 1943 attempt to assassinate

Hitler (he corresponded with Professor Emil Henk in this regard), to meet with the father of a young man beheaded for participating in the Munich student uprising of 1943, and to visit hospitals to which inmates from concentration camps had been moved.

In August 1945, Auden returned to New York City and to his work on *The Age of Anxiety*, which he finished in December 1946.

NOTES

1. W. H. Auden, "As Hateful Ares Bids," *The Commonweal*, Jan. 18, 1946, in W. H. Auden, *The Collected Works of W. H. Auden*, prose, vol. 2, ed. Edward Mendelson (Princeton, NJ: Princeton University Press, 2002), pp. 286–90.

2. Parker, 2004, p. 176, as quoted in James J. Berg and Chris Freeman, "Auden and Isherwood," in Tony Sharpe, ed., *W. H. Auden in Context* (New York: Cambridge University Press, 2013), pp. 316–25.

3. Auden's *Collected Poems* are dedicated to his two collaborators, Christopher Isherwood and Chester Kallman. *The Age of Anxiety* is dedicated to John Betjeman, who wrote a kind of topophiliac poetry about an England for which Auden remained nostalgic. See the essay Auden wrote about Betjeman during the time he was composing *The Age of Anxiety*: W. H. Auden, "Introduction to Slick but Not Streamlined, by John Betjeman," in Auden, *Collected Works*, vol. 2, pp. 303–07.

4. W. H. Auden, "The Public v. the Late Mr. William Butler Yeats," *Partisan Review*, Spring 1939, in Auden, *Collected Works*, vol. 2, p. 7.

5. Humphrey Carpenter, *W. H. Auden: A Biography* (Boston, MA: Houghton Mifflin, 1981), p. 8.

6. *Ibid.*, p. 9.

7. W. H. Auden, *Paid on Both Sides: A Charade*, in W. H. Auden, *Collected Poems* (London: Faber and Faber, 1976/1991), p. 16. See also John Fuller, *W. H. Auden: A Commentary* (London: Faber and Faber, 1998), p. 30.

8. W. H. Auden, "The Art of Healing: In Memoriam David Protetch, M.D.," Sept. 27, 1969, *The New Yorker*, p. 38, in Auden, *Collected Poems*, p. 835.

9. W. H. Auden, *Forewords & Afterwords* (New York: Vintage, 1997), p. 500.

10. W. H. Auden, British Library Add. MS. 52430, fol. 8, quoted in Carpenter, *W. H. Auden*, p. 11. Consider Auden's childhood ditty

about angels and shit in comparison to Jung's account of his childhood fantasy of God shitting on Basel Cathedral: "I gathered all my courage, as though I were about to leap forthwith into hell-fire, and let the thought come. I saw before me the cathedral, the blue sky. God sits on His golden throne high above the world—and from under the throne an enormous turd falls upon the sparkling new roof, shatters it, and breaks the walls of the cathedral asunder. See C. G. Jung, *Memories, Dreams, Reflections* (New York: Random House, 1961, Vintage, 1965), p. 29.

11. Gregory Bateson, "Double Bind Theory," *Steps Towards an Ecology of Mind: Collected Essays in Anthropology, Psychiatry, Evolution, and Epistemology* (Symposium on the Double Bind, 1969; Northvale, NJ: Jason Aronson Inc., 1972), pp. 276–83.

12. W. H. Auden, letter to James Stern, Jul. 30, 1942, quoted in W. H. Auden, *Juvenilia: Poems, 1922–1928*, ed. Katherine Bucknell (Princeton, NJ: Princeton University Press, 1994), p. xxix.

13. W. H. Auden, *The English Auden: Poems, Essays, and Dramatic Writings, 1927–1939*, ed. Edward Mendelson (New York: Random House, 1978), p. 359.

14. W. H. Auden, "New Year Letter," in *Auden, Collected Poems*, p. 108.

15. "In my case, it was Father who stood for the first, Mother for the second." W. H. Auden, "As It Seemed to Us" (1965), quoted in Auden, *Juvenilia*, p. xxxiv.

16. Christopher Isherwood, quoted in Edward Mendelson, "Auden and God," *The New York Review of Books*, Dec. 6, 2007, p. 3.

17. See Katherine Bucknell, "Introduction," in Auden, *Juvenilia*, p. xxii.

18. From *St. Edmund's School Chronicle*, June 1917, pp. 53–5, quoted in Carpenter, *W. H. Auden*, p. 18.

> No. 1 machine-gun, under Corpl. Auden (junior) [Wystan], was posted on the left ahead of his elder brother [John] and his patrol was connected with the centre by connecting files ... O. C. Red Force did a rather unwise thing. Being afraid of being cut off from the ridge to which he wished to retreat, he managed to get a message through to No. 1 gun to cover his retreat, and retired instantly by short rushes, some covering while others rushed (machine-gun fire did not seem to be forthcoming, but, as he learnt afterwards, Corpl. Auden (junior) was engaged on his own) ... Corpl. Auden (senior) then turned up and asked for advice. Corpl. Auden (junior) replied that the machine-gun was going to retire, and could he hold out a

> bit longer until he had reached the top and could cover his retreat. This was done, and then both turned their attention to the enemy's advance, and during the charge the Corporal gave them a good deal of lead, but was unable to stop them."

19. Carpenter, *W. H. Auden*, p. 31.

20. *Ibid.*, p. 28.

21. John Pudney, quoted in Carpenter, *W. H. Auden*, p. 45.

22. W. H. Auden, letter to James Stern, Jul. 30, 1942, quoted in Auden, *Juvenilia*, p. 1.

23. W. H. Auden, "The Watershed," in Auden, *Collected Poems*, pp. 32–33.

24. Letter to John Auden, letter to Christopher Isherwood, quoted in Auden, *Juvenilia*, p. xl.

25. Carpenter, *W. H. Auden*, p. 82.

26. Biographer Richard Davenport-Hines conjectures that the short trial of psychoanalysis was administered by the untrained Margaret Marshall, who treated and unsuccessfully married Auden's middle brother, John. Richard Davenport-Hines, "Auden's Life and Character," in Sharpe, *W. H. Auden in Context*, pp. 15–24. See also Richard Davenport-Hines, *Auden* (New York: Pantheon Books, 1995), pp. 70–74.

27. It may be useful to remember here that the English court convicted Oscar Wilde in 1895 for daring to speak of the love that had no name. *De Profundis*, his book-length letter about Eros, addressed to Lord Alfred Douglas and written during his years of hard labor in Reading Gaol, was published in England only in censored and abridged versions until as late as 1960. Homosexuality carried a prison sentence in Britain until 1967. In Berlin in 1928, police permitted the male brothels to operate, although the motivation for this control was far from altruistic.

28. Auden praised D. H. Lawrence's 1922 thesis that "the Western-romantic conception of personal love is a neurotic symptom, only inflaming our loneliness, a bad answer to our real wish to be united to and rooted in life." See Auden, *Collected Works*, vol. 2, p. 62. Elsewhere Auden writes,

> There are four things which Lawrence does supremely well: writing about non-human nature, writing as a stranger about places and people he sees for the first time, criticizing books, and describing states of irrational hostility between man and man or man and woman.

(W. H. Auden, "Some Notes on D. H. Lawrence," *The Nation*, Apr. 26, 1947, in Auden, *Collected Works*, vol. 2, p. 318.) But Auden described his own work, *The Orators*, as both his memorial to Lawrence and to the failure of the romantic conception of personality: "My guess today is that my unconscious motive in writing it was therapeutic, to exorcise certain tendencies in myself by allowing them to run riot in fantasy." W. H. Auden, *The Orators: An English Study* (London: Faber and Faber, 1966), p. 7.

29. For more information on John Layard, see Joel Weishaus's review of Layard's book, *The Snake, The Dragon, and the Tree* (2008) in *The International Journal of Jungian Studies* (IJJS). Accessed at http://www.cddc.vt.edu/host/weishaus/Writing/Layard.pdf.

30. In his essay, "The Ego and the Id" (1927), Freud cites Groddeck's *Book of the It* (1923) and takes up Groddeck's naming of that other part of the mind that behaves as if it were unconscious, the "id."

31. Alan Ansen, *The Table Talk of W. H. Auden*, ed. Nicholas Jenkins (Princeton, NJ: Ontario Review Press, 1990), p. 5.

32. W. H. Auden, "Letters from Iceland" (1936), in *The Collected Works of W. H. Auden*, prose, vol. 1, ed. Edward Mendelson (Princeton, NJ: Princeton University Press, 1997), p. 265.

33. W. H. Auden, "1929," in Auden, *Collected Poems*, p. 46.

34. W. H. Auden, "The Wanderer," in Auden, *Collected Poems*, p. 62.

35. W. H. Auden, "Consider This and in Our Time," in Auden, *Collected Poems*, p. 62.

36. W. H. Auden, "Poetry, Poets, and Taste" (1936), in Auden, *Collected Works*, vol. 1, pp. 162–65.

37. W. H. Auden, "A Summer Night" (1933), in Auden, *Collected Poems*, pp. 117–19.

See also W. H. Auden, "Introduction," in *The Protestant Mystics*, quoted in Edward Mendelson, *Early Auden* (London: Faber and Faber, 1981), pp. 160–61.

38. See Erika Mann, *School for Barbarians: Education Under the Nazis* (London: Lindsay Drummond Ltd., 1939).

39. W. H. Auden, Bodleian Library, Ms. Eng. Lett. C. 464, quoted in Mendelson, *Early Auden*, pp. 195–96.

40. George Orwell, 1940, "Inside the Whale," *Inside the Whale and Other Essays* (Harmondsworth: Penguin Books, 1957), pp. 36–7.

> The second stanza is intended as a sort of thumb-nail sketch of a day in the life of a 'good party-man.' In the morning a couple

of political murders, a ten-minutes' interlude to stifle 'bourgeois' remorse, and then a hurried luncheon and a busy afternoon and evening chalking walls and distributing leaflets. All very edifying. But notice the phrase 'necessary murders.' It could only be written by a person to whom murder is at most a word. Personally I would not speak so lightly of murder. It so happens that I have seen the bodies of numbers of murdered men—I don't mean killed in battle, I mean murdered. Therefore I have some conception of what murder means—the terror, the hatred, the howling relatives, the post-mortems, the blood, the smells. To me, murder is something to be avoided. So it is to the ordinary person. The Hitlers and Stalins find murder necessary, but they don't advertise their callousness, and they don't speak of it as murder; it is 'liquidation', 'elimination', or some other soothing phrase. Mr. Auden's brand of amoralism is only possible if you are the kind of person who is always somewhere else when the trigger is pulled. So much of left-wing thought is a kind of playing with fire by people who don't even know that fire is hot.

41. W. H. Auden, "Foreword" to the 1966 *Collected Shorter Poems*, quoted in John Fuller, *W. H. Auden: A Commentary* (London: Faber and Faber, 1998), p. 286.

42. W. H. Auden, "In Time of War," in Auden, *Collected Works*, vol. 1, pp. 674.

43. E. M. Forster, *Howard's End* (Harmondsworth: Penguin Classics, 1985), p. 316.

They laid Leonard, who was dead, on the gravel; Helen poured water over him.
'That's enough,' said Charles.
'Yes, murder's enough,' said Miss Avery, coming out of the house with the sword.

44. W. H. Auden, "In Time of War," (revised as "Sonnets from China," *Collected Poems*, pp. 183–95), in Auden, *Collected Works*, vol. 1, pp. 667–80.

45. W. H. Auden, Sonnet XVI, "In Time of War," in Auden, *Collected Works*, vol. 1, pp. 674.

46. Pat Barker's *Regeneration* trilogy of novels depicts in the first volume the psychiatrist W. H. R. Rivers employing Freudian techniques to treat the English poet Siegfried Sassoon for shell shock. In the third volume, Rivers re-examines his medical war work in the light of his earlier anthropological investigations into the warring culture on the island of Melanesia. Pat Barker, *Regeneration, The Eye*

in the Door, and *The Ghost Road* (New York: Viking Press, 1991, 1993, 1995).

47. Auden writes, "The verse Commentary is, I know, far too 'preachy' in manner and, were I to preach the same sermon today, I should do it very differently. I have always believed, however, that, among the many functions of the poet, preaching is one." Auden, *Collected Works*, vol. 1, p. 830. In a letter to E. R. Dodds, he admits, "I am very uncertain whether this kind of thing is possible without becoming a prosy pompous old bore." Fuller, *W. H. Auden*, p. 244.

48. Carpenter, *W. H. Auden*, p. 243.

49. W. H. Auden, "The Sportsmen" (1938), in Auden, *Collected Works*, vol. 1, pp. 455–57.

50. W. H. Auden, "Democracy's Reply to the Challenge of Dictators" (1939), in Auden, *Collected Works*, vol. 1, p. 466.

51. W. H. Auden, quoted in John Matthias, *Reading Old Friends: Essays, Reviews, and Poems on Poetics, 1975–1990*, SUNY Press, 1992, p. 98, in Stan Smith, "Ideas About England," in Sharpe, *W. H. Auden in Context*, p. 45.

52. W. H. Auden, "In Memory of W. B. Yeats," *Collected Poems*, pp. 247–49.

53. Richard Davenport-Hines, *Auden*, (New York: Pantheon Books, 1995), p. 186.

54. W. H. Auden, letters to A. E. Dodds, Jul. 11, 1939 and May 1939, quoted in Carpenter, *W. H. Auden*, p. 256.

55. W. H. Auden, letter to Stephen Spender, quoted in Mendelson, *Early Auden*, p. 206; see also Stan Smith, *The Cambridge Companion to W. H. Auden* (Cambridge: Cambridge University Press, 2004), p. 2.

56. In his letter to E. R. Dodds, Jun. 27, 1940, Auden quotes from Vaslav Nijinsky, *The Diary of Vaslav Nijinsky* (London: Victor Gollancz, 1937), p. 44; see also Fuller, *W. H. Auden*, p. 291.

57. The quotation can be found in a slightly different translation (by Kyril Fitzlyon in *The Diary of Vaslav Nijinsky*, 1999): "Lloyd George is a hypocrite. Lloyd George is Diaghilev. Diaghilev does not want love for everyone. Diaghilev wants love for himself. I want love toward everyone." Vaslav Nijinsky, *The Diary of Vaslav Nijinsky*, trans. Kyril Fitzlyon (Chicago, IL: University of Illinois Press, 2006), p. 64.

58. Fuller, *W. H. Auden*, p. 291.

59. W. H. Auden, Foreword to Bloomfield's *Bibliography*, in Fuller, *W. H. Auden*, p. 292.

Rereading a poem of mine, 1ˢᵗ September 1939, after it had been
published, I came to the line, "We must love one another or die,'
and said to myself: 'That's a damn lie! We must die anyway.' So,
in the next edition, I altered it to 'We must love one another and
die.' This didn't seem to do either, so I cut the stanza. Still no
good. The whole poem, I realized, was infected with an incurable
dishonesty—and must be scrapped.

60. Carpenter, *W. H. Auden*, p. 282.

61. See W. H. Auden, The Prolific and the Devourer (draft), in
Auden, *Collected Works*, vol. 2, pp. 409–58.

62. P. N. Furbank, *E. M. Forster: A Life* (New York: Harcourt
Brace Jovanovich, 1978), p. 238.

On June 13, 1940, a question was asked in the British Parliament
about the war service of Auden and Isherwood, and the next
day the *Spectator* printed a vicious epigram, penned by W.
R. Matthews, the Dean of St. Paul's, addressed 'To Certain
Intellectuals Safe in America': 'This Europe stinks,' you cried—
swift to desert / Your stricken country in her sore distress. / You
may not care, but still I will assert / Since you have left us, here
the stink is less.

63. Auden, "New Year Letter," *Collected Poems*, p. 206.

64. *Ibid.*, p. 201.

65. *Ibid.*, p. 208. When Auden arrived in New York City at the
beginning of 1939, he met (through his wife Erika Mann) and very
much admired Wolfgang Köhler, the creator of Gestalt psychology,
recently escaped from Nazi Germany. In a letter to A. E. Dodds,
Auden described Köhler, who eventually taught as faculty member
at Swarthmore College as "one of the great men I've ever met." See
Carpenter, *W. H. Auden*, p. 253.

66. "Compelling all to the admission / Aloneness is man's real
condition, / That each must travel forth alone / In search of the
Essential Stone." Auden, "New Year Letter," *Collected Poems*, p. 238.

67. *Ibid.*, pp. 212–13.

68. Matthew 5: 9. Jesus meets the man from Gadara who is
possessed by devils.

69. In *Secondary Worlds* (1968), Auden will differentiate between
the white magic of poetry and the black magic of propaganda that
practices enchantment as a way to dominate. See Stan Smith, *The
Cambridge Companion to W. H. Auden* (Cambridge: Cambridge
University Press, 2004), p. 3.

70. Edward Mendelson, *Later Auden* (New York: Farrar Straus and Giroux, 1999), p. 101. See also W. H. Auden, "Balaam and His Ass," in *The Collected Works of W. H. Auden*, prose, vol. 3, ed. Edward Mendelson (Princeton, NJ: Princeton University Press, 2008), pp. 444–71; see also Rainer Emig, "Auden in German," in Sharpe, *W. H. Auden in Context*, pp. 306–15.

71. Auden, "New Year Letter," *Collected Poems*, p. 206.

72. *Ibid.*, p. 238.

73. *Ibid.*, p. 206.

74. In November 1939, Auden wrote an elegy for Freud, who died in exile in London on September 23, 1939, calling Eros the "builder of Cities" (*Collected Poems*, p. 276). But Freud introduced the word *Eros* into his authorized vocabulary very late in his practice, in *Beyond the Pleasure Principle* (1920). In 1921, he wrote,

> Anyone who considers sex as something mortifying and humiliating to human nature is at liberty to make use of the more genteel expressions 'Eros' and 'erotic.' I might have done so myself from the first and thus have spared myself much opposition. But I did not want to, for I like to avoid concessions to faintheartedness. One can never tell where that road may lead one: one gives way first in words, and then little by little in substance too.

Sigmund Freud, *Group Psychology and the Analysis of the Ego* (1921), in *The Standard Edition of the Complete Psychological Works of Sigmund Freud*, vol. XVIII (London: Hogarth Press, 1955), p. 91; see also J. Laplanche and J. B. Pontalis, *The Language of Psychoanalysis*, trans. Donald Nicholson-Smith (London: Karnac, 1973/2004), pp. 153–54.

75. Mendelson, *Later Auden*, p. 104.

76. Allen Ginsberg, "...'This is the Abomination,'" *The Colombia Review*, May 1946, p. 163, in Aidan Wasley, *The Age of Auden: Postwar Poetry and the American Scene* (Princeton, NJ: Princeton University Press, 2011), p. 34.

> Auden's poetry has always aroused much interest, the more so because Auden's personality and technique and opinions have been so flexible. He has been consistently evolving toward disciplined, responsible utterance, and away from slipshod emotional crisis, over-conscious penitence, tender despondency, and nostalgia. *Another Time* and *New Year Letter* assume power as statements of transition to mastery of personal sorrow and insight into general terror. The tentative accomplishment of this maturity, in *For the*

> *Time Being*, set it apart as one of the few great works of poetry of our time, rivaled only by Eliot's last book of poetry and his plays. A definitive review of *For the Time Being* is impossible; it is the kind of book that reviews the reviewer: it is too intelligent in thought and perfected in techniques to allow immediate formal judgment. A full appreciation, exegesis, and criticism must be left to the literary studies which will come.

Wasley points out (p. 47) that William Burroughs was the first person to give Ginsberg a volume of Auden's poems, and in 1947 it was Auden's poem, *The Age of Anxiety*, that provided the inspiration for the Beat-friendly avant-garde magazine, *Neurotica*, with its editorial ethos of angst and cultural unease.

77. W. H. Auden, Contribution to *Modern Canterbury Pilgrims*, in Auden, *Collected Works*, vol. 3, pp. 573–80.

78. "*A Christmas Oratorio* is the only direct treatment of sacred subjects I shall ever attempt. My mother had just died, and I wanted to write something for her." Alan Ansen, *The Table Talk of W. H. Auden*, ed. Nicholas Jenkins (Princeton, NJ: Ontario Review Press, 1990), p. 3. See also Fuller, *W. H. Auden*, p. 346.

79. Ansen, *The Table Talk*, p. 58. See also Seamus Perry, "Auden's Forms," in Sharpe, *W. H. Auden in Context*, p. 387.

80. In his last year of school at Gresham's, Auden played Caliban in a school production of *The Tempest*. "This was his own choice—he had made a special effort to be selected for it—and he gave a remarkable performance." Carpenter, *W. H. Auden*, p. 41.

81. W. H. Auden, "The Cave of Making," *Collected Poems*, p. 692.

82. W. H. Auden, "W. H. Auden Speaks of Poetry and Total War," *The Chicago Sun*, Mar. 14, 1942, in Auden, *Collected Works*, vol. 2, pp. 152–53. See also Patrick Deer, "Auden and Wars," in Sharpe, *W. H. Auden in Context*, pp. 150–59.

83. W. H. Auden, quoted in Stephen Spender, ed., *W. H. Auden: A Tribute* (Worthing: Littlehampton Books Services, 1975), p. 136.

84. Auden's federal service records can be accessed at the National Archives. Unfortunately, his reports for the Morale Division of the United States Strategic Bombing Survey remain lost in the National Archives because these records were never filed by the reporting officer's name.

85. *New York Times Magazine*, Aug. 8, 1971, 10 ff; *Time* interview (unpublished) by T. G. Foote, 1963. See Carpenter, *W. H. Auden*, p. 243; Auden wrote very little about his experiences working for the War

Department. The best descriptions can be found in his friend James Stern's book, *The Hidden Damage*, in which Auden appears from time to time. In the same way that one reads Louis MacNeice and Auden's *Letters from Iceland* and Christopher Isherwood and Auden's *Journey to a War*, one can read Stern's *The Hidden Damage* and Auden's *The Age of Anxiety* as companion "takes" on a place and time. See James Stern, *The Hidden Damage* (New York: Harcourt Brace, 1947).

Figure 1: Auden, January 1, 1946, LIFE Collection, Getty Images.

CHAPTER TWO

AUDEN'S USE OF JUNG'S TYPOLOGY

A uden often worked mimetically, gathering together ideas and styles, extracting what he liked, and synthesizing these into something of his own. Some critics regarded this as an indication of Auden's breadth of knowledge; others dismissed it as the derivative thinking of a magpie.[1] Auden acknowledged Dante, William Langland (author of the fourteenth century dream vision poem *Piers Plowman*), Alexander Pope, and Thomas Hardy as his literary mentors.[2] His early philosophical and psychological sources included Marx and Freud, as well as Georg Groddeck, D. H. Lawrence, and Homer Lane. In New York, he was reading, among other authors, Søren Kierkegaard, Reinhold Niebuhr (on Christian ethics), Paul Tillich, and Jung.

Auden knew Jung's analytical psychology from very early on.[3] John Fuller, the magnificently well-read critic who has tracked and identified Auden's sources and influences, finds traces of Jung in a poem written when Auden was only twenty years old. "The four [who] sat on in the bare room" (1927), he points out, is an allegorical representation of Jung's four psychological functions co-existing in one mind, lodged in a single skull.[4] Having read Jung's 1928 essay, "On Psychical Energy," Auden depicts the phantoms in his 1929 poem "Family Ghosts" as Jung's unconscious complexes, transmitted inter-generationally like the curse of the house of Atreus.[5] Auden refers to these complexes manifesting as "archaic imagery"; the unconscious libidinal energy associated with them flows along deep pathways that function like an incline, gradient, or "watercourse" while the split-off dry and despairing conscious ego position hardens into an "Age of Ice." Fuller also argues that Auden deliberately structured the climbing party of four characters in the play *Ascent of F6* (written with Christopher Isherwood in 1936) on Jung's types. Certainly, at the end of his 1935 essay "Psychology and Art Today," Auden includes in his list of "Books to Read" two works by Jung: *Psychology of the Unconscious* and *Two Essays on Analytical Psychology.*⁶

Jung called the psychological concept of the unconscious the "shadow," a personification that Auden found useful. For instance, in the sonnet sequence "In Time of War" in *Journey to a War* (1938), Auden describes the defeated in terms of both shadow and anxiety: "Loss is their shadow-wife, Anxiety / Receives them like a grand hotel."⁷ In his eulogy "In Memory of Ernst Toller," first published in *The New Yorker* on June 17, 1939, Auden speaks directly to the Expressionist playwright who fled from Nazi Germany to New York and then hanged himself on May 22, 1939. The central metaphor of the poem is of shadow: the shadows of the mourners that chase them from the grave, the shadow of Ernst Toller that "unwittingly" spoke, and the now shadowless man whom the poet-speaker hopes to lay to rest. About this predominant shadowy unconscious, Auden writes, "We are lived by powers we pretend to understand" and, ominously in a poem about suicide, "they direct at the end ... even our hand."⁸ Curiously, Fuller attributes Auden's reference to "powers" in this poem only to Groddeck's concept of the Id/It, even though Jung's concept of the unconscious as "shadow" is the extended organizing metaphor of the entire poem.⁹

Six months after this elegy, Auden published a review of Walter de la Mare's book *Behold, This Dreamer*. "In the last analysis we *are* lived, for the night brings forth the day," he says, an expression very similar to the conclusion of his poem for Ernst Toller. Auden expresses puzzlement that de la Mare's book about dreams omits Jung. Indeed, he compensates for this omission by defining the difficulty at the heart of de la Mare's book with a distinctively Jungian vocabulary:

> For the problem which [the book] raises and in part helps to solve
> is of much wider importance than questions of literary taste, even
> if it perhaps immediately concerns writers more than most people,
> namely: What attitude should we adopt to that half of life which
> dominates the night, to the Unconscious, the Instinctive and extra-
> personal, the Determined, the Daemonic? ... The daemon creates

> Jacob the prudent Ego, not for the latter to lead, in self-isolation
> and contempt, a frozen attic life of its own, but to be a loving and
> reverent antagonist; for it is only through that wrestling bout of
> which the sex act and the mystical union are the typical symbols
> that the future is born, that Jacob acquires the power and the will
> to live, and the demon is transformed into an angel.[10]

The review concludes with the depiction of the dynamic between conscious and unconscious as the wrestling of Jacob and the angel in Genesis 32:21–31. Jacob and the daemonic, as well as the transformation of demon into angel, are references that neither Groddeck in *Exploring the Unconscious* and *The World of Man* nor Freud in his *Standard Edition of the Complete Psychological Works* ever employed, but Jung took up both references in his early work, *Symbols of Transformation* (1912), as well as in a much later essay, "The Phenomenology of the Spirit in Fairy Tales" (1945).[11]

Auden often referred to the shadow as "lame," as an inferior part of the personality that manifests in uncontrolled emotions. Auden first learned about the shadow from John Layard, who, after a suicide attempt in Berlin, underwent Jungian analysis. In a letter, Auden thanks Layard, and he depicts his own inferior function as affectionately released when he fell in love with Chester Kallman in 1939. "My dear old Lame Shadow," he told Layard, "puts its arms around my neck and says, 'Thank you. You *have* been an old Bore, you know, but let's forget about that. Now I can fly back to Heaven where I belong. So long. Remember me to John Layard. I always liked that man.'"[12] Likewise, in his essay, "Eros and Agape," a review of *Love in the Western World* by Denis de Rougemont, Auden refers to the problem of the shadow within the Western social institution of marriage:

> It is only in the past hundred years that people have seriously
> tried to marry their mater-imagos on their Lame-Shadows, and it
> is only quite recently that, dismayed at the failure of this attempt,
> they have denied the significance of personal relations altogether
> and returned to a collective and political myth of Eros.[13]

Between 1939 and 1941, Auden collaborated with Benjamin Britten on the opera *Paul Bunyan*. Auden's libretto calls the figures in a Greek chorus "Lame Shadows and Animas." In an article about his version of *Paul Bunyan* entitled "Opera on an American Legend," Auden identifies the blue ox Babe as a symbol of Paul Bunyan's anima, his advisor, his soul-image, the archetype of life, quite distinct from the lumberjack's wife, with whom Paul fails to get on.[14] Four characters in *Paul Bunyan* may also prefigure Auden's dramatization of Jung's psychological types in *The Age of Anxiety*: the Alaskan gold speculator as Intuition, the Western gunman as Sensation, the Alabaman suicide (the only female character of the four) as Feeling, and the Wall Street speculator as Thought.[15]

Auden's use of Jung's typology became even more explicit in the Christmas oratorio *For the Time Being*, finished in 1942. At the beginning of the section of the poem entitled "The Annunciation," the "Four Faculties" speak. They are Intuition, who resembles a dwarf in the belly; Feeling, like a nymph in the heart; Sensation, like a giant at the gates; and Thought, fairy-like and disembodied in the human brain. Together, they speak as a fragmented Many, sundered and expelled from the Oneness of the personality as a result of the Fall and the Expulsion from Eden. Auden dramatizes them as exclusive, partial, and each longing nostalgically for the wholeness of the garden that they can still glimpse, each in its own fashion. They bear witness to the fallen world that they describe as a "raging landscape," as a "sombre valley of an industry in dereliction" that is peopled by human beings both unconscious and without insight. And then the angel Gabriel arrives, approaches Mary, and utters the word, "Wake."[16]

Auden found Jung's typology meaningful in his discussions about his own psychological orientation and those of his family and friends. He identified himself as introverted and spoke of the difficulties of the English boarding school experience, of feeling condemned to spend every minute at close quarters with other people when he really required solitude in order to feel like himself.[17] He also compared Jung's critical psychology of types to William Blake's poetic vision of the human as a unity consisting of infinite emanations of being.

> Now I know that introverts and extroverts, like Blake's Prolifics
> and Devourers, are irreconcilable antagonists, but both equally
> necessary to existence, that both have essential contributions
> to make towards the enriching and improvement of human life,
> that both are threatened by different kinds of dangers to be
> met in different kinds of ways, and that the attempt, founded
> on envy of the one to imitate the other is always a disastrous
> failure for all.[18]

Auden described himself as an Introverted Thinking-Intuitive type. He hypothesized that he may have shared this psychological orientation with his mother, while, according to his assessment, his father was a Feeling-Sensation type. In his essay, "A Literary

Transference," he describes the writer Thomas Hardy serving for him not only as the archetype of the Poetic but also as a literary father-substitute: "To begin with, he [Hardy] looked like my father: that broad unpampered moustache, bald forehead, and deeply lined sympathetic face belonged to the other world of feeling and sensation (for I, like my mother, was a thinking-intuitive)." He was not blind to Hardy's faults, among them sentimentality and a tedious style, but, compared with his own, Hardy's emotions were "deeper and more faithful" and his "attachment to the earth ... more secure and observant." Believing himself to be both more detached and less temperamental, he wished he could experience emotion as fully as Hardy evidently could.[19]

In an introduction to *Tales of Grimm and Andersen*, Auden observed that, to an introverted child like he was, a water turbine could be as enchanting as any fairy-tale creature.[20] He often reflected on his childhood as indicative of his psychological orientation: "I spent a great many of my waking hours in the construction and elaboration of a private sacred world, the basic elements of which were a landscape, northern and limestone, and an industry, lead mining."[21] In this imaginary setting, he was the "sole autocrat." He experienced the technical vocabulary of mining and the geological terms relating to mining as numinous, as religious, and ignorance of them as "impiety."[22] At the same time, he had no practical mechanical ability nor any interest whatsoever in actual mining. The machinery, the tunnels, the geological information, all attracted him because of their names and because they were symbols of something subterranean and other-worldly, something both precise and unfathomable. He concluded, "I doubt if a person with both these passions, for the word and for the symbol, could become anything but a poet."[23]

Looking back on childhood, Auden regarded his experiences as already strongly skewed. For instance, he recalled a friend's daring and agility in jumping from a high diving board into a swimming pool. The young Auden could muster neither the courage nor the fortitude to attempt it alone, but he convinced his friend to jump into the pool with Auden on his back. When they hit the water, Auden didn't let go. The impact and the young Auden's physical ineptness combined; he hit his face on the back of his friend's head, and, to the shock of spectators, he surfaced bleeding. As an adult, Auden told this story to show that, in trying to escape his psychological orientation by riding on the back of his opposite, he came up with a bloody nose.[24]

At the same time, Auden described sometimes experiencing his superior functions—auxiliary intuition framed within superior thinking, in traditionally structured word-anchored forms—as powerfully oracular. In a transcribed conversation, he designated two instances when prophetic foresight manifested as pure accident in his writing. In 1934, he quite naturally included in his poem "A Bride in the 30s" the names of Hitler, Mussolini, and Roosevelt, but he also included Churchill, who, at this time, was only a newly elected Member of Parliament.[25] A few years later, in 1938, aboard a ship in the Mediterranean on the way to China, he wrote "O Tell Me the Truth about Love." The poem was very important to him, an importance that his companion Christopher Isherwood spotted at once. Soon afterwards, Auden met Kallman and fell deeply in love in an epiphany of eros comparable to his 1933 vision of agape.

Figure 2: Auden and Chester Kallman, PEN Conference, Venice, 1949. Bridgeman Images.

Auden's understanding of Jung's typology changed just before the composition of *The Age of Anxiety*. In 1940, Auden wrote to Stephen Spender: "My dominant faculties are intellect and intuition, my weak ones feeling and sensation. This means I have to approach life via the former; I must have knowledge and a great deal of it before I can feel anything."[26] Here Auden defines his personal equation and, a bit optimistically, pictures himself working through his superior function to access his inferior function, a psychological feat that, according to Jung himself, would be most unlikely. But in a letter written in 1942 to Spender, Auden wrote very differently:

> The next step for us, as poets, lies in opposite directions. You have to get over your camp of pity and accept your strength, I over my camp of tough aggressiveness, and accept my weakness. I.e., your poetry has to lose its whiff of the yearning school-girl, and mine its whiff of the hearty scoutmaster. Technically this probably means that I should deprive myself of the support of strict conventional forms, while you should impose them on yourself, in other words, we should both attempt the difficult (for us each).[27]

This 1942 letter marked an important reversal, an admonition that the difficult way forward required that he acknowledge the limits of his ego consciousness, identified with his earnest intellect, and accept the value of what he experienced as his inferior psychological functioning in sensation and feeling.[28]

What had happened between the two letters of 1940 and 1942? The thirty-seven-year-old Auden referred to it as "The Crisis" of his life. In January 1941, Auden composed a poem for Kallman's nineteenth birthday, in which he, as an Introverted Thinking-Intuitive type, warns Kallman of the needs and dangers of being an Introverted Thinking-Sensation type:

> So, Chester, let's open our gay celebrations
>   By wishing you luck in your twentieth year ...
>
> So much would occur to a sensitive stranger,
>   But friends must get down to the Particular;
> O what are the needs and what are the dangers
>   For the Thinking-Sensation Type that you are?
>
> Thought can be led to dogmatic abuses;
>   A theory's a tool to reject when it's broke:
> So consider them all as just gifts from the Muses
>   Who are charming but fond of a practical joke.
>
> Sensation that in the Gestalt of a city
>   Can see the Concrete in its multiple parts,
> You can train it on music, but I think it's a pity
>   If it's quite untrained in the Visual Arts.
>
> In harness the Two are a fine combination
>   But a little too fond of the mirror—Beware

When you look in one then of the fair fascination
  Provided by that ingenious pair.

Remember that poor old Lame Shadow—that other
  Neglected child in his jealousy;
Must he always be conscious of missing his mother?
  O learn Feeling from Elsie, Intuition from me.

And for all of us here, let me ask in conclusion
  That our wishes be horses and do as they're bid;
Success to the happy and loving, confusion
  To Political Parties, Policemen, and Sid.[29]

And a message to all in the States where they're apt to
  Believe in the Tough and the Real—I say NERTS:
Considering the world that we have to adapt to
  We can thank our stars if we're introverts.[30]

Six months later, in July 1941, Kallman revealed that he had been
sexually unfaithful and decided to end that aspect of his relations with
Auden. For Auden, this love for Kallman that had been intuited on the
boat to China, sparked on first meeting just after arriving in New York,
experienced as a vision of eros as palpable and lucid as his vision of
agape in 1933, and then realized with intimate time together almost
every day for two years, was sacramental, a marriage. But now it would
not be reciprocated in the way he had fervently wished. Kallman's
infidelities and his sexual withdrawal made Auden experience for the
first time in his life what he had reported in Spain, in China, in the
Yorkville cinema, in the lives of others: a blinding murderous rage.
Apparently, Auden half-attempted to strangle Kallman in his sleep.
Hateful Ares, the eristic impulse, possessed him utterly. Auden was
still overwrought when he wrote to Kallman at Christmas 1941:
"On account of you, I have been, in intention, and almost in act, a
murderer." Fifteen years later, Auden said, "I was forced to know in
person what it is like to feel oneself the prey of demonic powers, in
both the Greek and Christian sense, stripped of self-control and self-
respect, behaving like a ham-actor in a Strindberg play."[31]

Auden took seriously the dialectic between his art and his life and
the integrity that this demanded. In a commencement address given
at Smith College in August 1940, Auden critiqued Romanticism and
quoted Jung on the problem of the collective shadow.

> The dominant intellectual romanticism of this century has so
> possessed us that Jung hardly went far enough when he said, 'Hitler

> is the unconscious of every German; he comes uncomfortably near
> being the unconscious of most of us.' The shock of discovering
> through Freud and Marx that when we thought we were being
> perfectly responsible, logical, and loving we were nothing of the
> kind, has led us to believe that responsibility and logic and love
> are meaningless words; instead of bringing us to repentance, it
> has brought us to a nihilistic despair.[32]

A year later, Auden was struggling personally to understand how he had convinced himself that, in his relationship with Kallman, he had been perfectly responsible, logical, and loving, only to find that, however unconsciously, he had been destructive, paternalistic, and domineering towards an intelligent, if masochistic and immature, young man. The crisis broke Auden and catapulted him into the Slough of Despond.

From there, not only Romanticism had to be scrutinized and rejected. By 1942 Auden expressed increasing skepticism about orthodox psychoanalysis itself, in which he had invested so much faith in earlier times. Psychoanalysis could disenchant in the sense that one gave up neurotic evasion and resigned oneself to living as an adult bereft, but Auden noted that the void created by that disenchantment made one potentially even more vulnerable to negative possession.

> Psychoanalysis, like all pagan *scientia*, says: 'Come, my good
> man, no wonder you feel guilty. You have a distorting mirror,
> and that is indeed a very wicked thing to have. But cheer up.
> For a trifling consideration I shall be delighted to straighten it
> out for you. There. Look. A perfect image. The evil of distortion
> is exorcised. Now you have nothing to repent of any longer.
> Now you are one of the illumined and the elect. That will be ten
> thousand dollars, please.'
>
> And immediately come seven devils, and the last state of that man
> is worse than the first.[33]

Within the context of world war, as well as the more intimate context of his personal crisis with Kallman, Auden rejected orthodox psychoanalysis for not providing a strong enough counter-response to the eristic impulse.

About this rejection, critic Alan Jacobs expresses surprise: "It is strange to see Auden treating psychoanalysis so skeptically, since at the very time he wrote these words he was drawing regularly—especially in his verse—on the work of Carl Gustav Jung." Here, Jacobs presents psychoanalysis and analytical psychology as synonymous; he does not acknowledge the historical, theoretical, and practical differences between these schools of thought and practice, even though Auden apparently did differentiate between them. But Auden was never really devoted to Jung's theorizing, as he had been to Freud as a thinker, and his dismissal of psychoanalysis signified the loss of a paternal healer figure clustered around the father imago in his psyche. Shallow as Jacobs's perception of Auden's understanding of analytical psychology may be, though, it leads him to an important observation: "Instead, he discovered in Jung a rich conceptual vocabulary that could be applied to many of Auden's key concerns. Jung's account of myth and archetype would provide a way for Auden to talk about the power of poetry and story for the rest of his life."[34]

It would be simplistic and misleading to argue that Auden rejected Freud and became Jungian. In the 1940s, Kierkegaard, not Jung, served as Auden's Virgil through the purgatory of the spurned lover, to say nothing of the witness to war.[35] Kierkegaard interpreted a love problem neither as an aesthetic problem (is it interesting?) nor as an ethical problem (is it good or bad?), but as a religious problem to be consciously suffered; the sufferer must accept the suffering and forgive his betrayer. In 1944, in "A Preface to Kierkegaard," Auden wrote, "Kierkegaard considers the erotic relation and is concerned to show that, for an individual who has once been exposed to Christianity, there are, irrespective of his or her belief, only three possibilities: marriage; celibacy … ; and despair."[36] Resigning himself to remain despairingly in the relationship with Kallman, he became "anxious" in the Kierkegaardian religious sense of consciously enduring that suffering from the perspective of a many-voiced, gathered-together individual human being.[37] Auden and Kallman did not resume sexual relations, but they remained companions and, from 1953 until Auden's death in 1973, housemates.

When Auden took up his war-work in New York between 1939 and 1945, all these elements came together in four major formulations. As I mentioned in the previous chapter, *New Year Letter* defined the dilemma in a personal epistle shaped as an epic question: "to what conditions must we bow / in building the Just City now?" *For the Time Being* examined this question about the human condition in terms of religion, the dialectic between the demands of the Eternal and the individual in time. *The Sea and the Mirror* addressed the same in terms of art and its relation to life. And then as he began to compose *The Age of Anxiety*, he stepped into weakness—into his anxiety—as well as engaging the strength of his past thinking, and he hypothesized the following:

> The basic human problem is man's anxiety in time: e.g., his present anxiety over himself in relation to his past and his parents (Freud), his present anxiety over himself in relation to his future and his neighbors (Marx), his present anxiety over himself in relation to eternity and God (Kierkegaard).[38]

Auden defined anxiety in the ideas of these three writers, but he approached it artistically in terms proposed by a fourth, Jung. He grounded his question about anxiety in the physical context of New York during war time. Psychologically, he devised the poem as a dialectic within intrapsychic consciousness itself, as defined by Jung. Auden employed poetic form in a manner analogous to how psychotherapists employ frame. He began by drawing a circumference around his subject matter, delineating a poetic *temenos* of rhythm, rhyme, and traditional narrative form around the field of his subjective theme of anxiety. Only then did he open himself to the emerging words and symbols, images and emotions, to both the destructive element and the creative, constructive impulse sparked within the space.[39] Psychotherapists know that to constellate unconscious processes in patients without a psychotherapeutic frame is counter-productive, even dangerous.[40] Auden had known something similar about his creative process as early as 1931, when he wrote, "In general the further away from you in time or feeling that poets are, the more you can get out of them for your own use. Often some piece of technique thus learnt really unchains one's own Daimon quite suddenly."[41] For *The Age of Anxiety*, he chose the distance and artifice of an archaic alliterative verse style and a classical narrative form as his artistic frame. Stepping into the framed allegorical field of *psychomachia* or internal warfare,[42] he took as his compass the four-part typological template that Jung defined as four psychological functions in their combinations with two psychological attitudes.[43]

In 1946, in the midst of writing *The Age of Anxiety*, Auden entered into an intimate, including sexual, relationship with a woman named Rhoda Jaffe. She had known Auden since his first months in New York, was friendly with Kallman at Brooklyn College, and had completed some secretarial work for Auden. Her marriage had failed, and she had been trying to talk Auden into a sexual liaison for some time. The affair did not change Auden's sexual orientation, but Jaffe's affection altered him deeply, fundamentally.[44] It also radically influenced the narrative outcome of his poem.

Figure 3: Auden and Rhoda Jaffe, Bridgeman Images.

Auden sets *The Age of Anxiety* in a bar on Third Avenue during the war on the night of the Feast of All Souls. All Hallows Eve on October 31 is a pagan celebration of shadowy spirits, and the Feast of All Saints on November 1 honors the lives of the saints. In the Catholic and High Anglican calendars, on November 2 the living commemorate and pray for all the faithful dead who must spend time in Purgatory expiating their sins before entering heaven. Setting the poem on All Souls, Auden positions his narrative in the tradition of Dante and in an allegorical context of purgation, of suffering and possible cleansing; the eternally damned populate Dante's *Inferno*, but his *Purgatorio* maps the ascent of good Christians through seven circles of penance into Paradise.

Auden's poem begins with a Prologue, which is followed by four movements or narratives: "The Seven Ages," "The Seven Stages," "The Dirge," and "The Masque." In each of these sections, the four characters relate to each other in varying combinations and settings.

Finally, in the Epilogue, they again separate. Throughout, the narrating voice describes and comments on their actions.

In the Prologue, the narrator introduces the *dramatis personae*: four protagonists, each sitting separately. Quant looks at his tired reflection in the mirror behind the bar. In public life, he's a widowed middle-aged clerk in a shipping office near the Battery. More privately, he's an Irish immigrant who came to America at the age of six and who remembers sitting in a public library through a winter during the Depression, unemployed, reading mythology; he carries that knowledge like heavy unopened baggage. He is Intuition. Malin, watching the bubbles rise in his glass, exhausted by the practical demands of his work as a Medical Intelligence Officer in the Canadian Air Force, also reminisces, in his case about the past pleasures of studying at university. He is Thinking. Rosetta, a successful buyer in a department store, experienced with but disappointed by men, amuses herself with a favorite daydream based on her childhood in England: the innocent, ordered green countryside of detective novels, with just the hint of a corpse hidden in the bushes. She is Feeling. Emble, a Mid-Westerner now serving in the Navy, looks around the bar, conscious of how his uniform attracts both sexes, and he responds with contempt when he receives an admiring glance, with irritation when he doesn't. He is Sensation.[45]

A radio in the bar interrupts the four interior monologues with loud reports from "the common world of great slaughter and much sorrow." The bad news stirs the four strangers to recognize their common humanity.[46] At Rosetta's suggestion, they shift from their bar stools to the quieter intimacy of a booth and begin to chat.

The title of the first main movement, "The Seven Ages," refers to the famous soliloquy, "All the world's a stage," in Shakespeare's *As You Like It*, in which Jaques describes the life span of a human being. By temperament, Jaques is a melancholic, and his summation of the seven ages of a human life is grim: "At first, the infant / Mewling and puking in the nurse's arms," then whining school boy, woeful lover, vainglorious soldier, pontificating judge, shrunken old man, and finally "second childishness and mere oblivion, / Sans teeth, sans eyes, sans taste, sans everything."[47] Auden's more complex version of the Seven Ages braids together the conscious functioning of all four protagonists in conversation. In his essays and reviews Auden argued rigorously from a single intellectual standpoint, but he was convinced that poetic truth required many voices. In "The Seven Ages," for each of the phases of a human life, Malin as Thinking begins to speak, and then the other characters riff off Malin's statement with their own associations and impressions.[48]

But, of course, as in the Shakespearean soliloquy, any narrative sequence of a lifespan necessarily moves forward in time towards images of personal "extinction." After a pause during which Malin goes to the men's room and Quant to the bar to fetch more drinks, the second movement, "The Seven Stages," begins. The conversation moves toward greater complexity and depth. Quant (the Intuitive) asks Rosetta (the Feeling function) to guide them into a different narrative, in search of "hope and health." Rosetta agrees to start off a shared narrative of Seven Stages en route to "The Quiet Kingdom," although she qualifies their hungry hopes by saying, perhaps ironically, "May our luck find the / Regressive road to Grandmother's House" (p. 56). I say "ironically," because she signals that traditional dream-quest narratives inevitably move "regressively," backwards through time, toward something archaic and collective, toward what she calls "Grandmother's House," to what Charles Perrault cast as a devouring wolf disguised and waiting in the Grandmother's bed, to what Goethe called the "Mothers." But the others don't register Rosetta's wish for "luck." Certainly, the narrator observes that the four protagonists feel emboldened by their commiseration and by their drinking. The narrator says,

> For it can happen, if circumstances are otherwise propitious, that members of a group in this condition [of semi-intoxication] establish a rapport in which communication of thoughts and feelings is so accurate and instantaneous, that they appear to function as a single organism. ... The more completely these four forgot their surroundings and lost their sense of time, the more sensitively aware of each other they became, until they achieved in their dream that rare community which is otherwise only attained in states of extreme wakefulness. (p. 57)

Auden models "The Seven Stages" on the medieval dream quest narrative. His favorite poem, Dante's *Divine Comedy*, is an example; his favorite poem in alliterative verse, Langland's *Piers Plowman*, is another.[49] In an essay written at this time, Auden observes:

> The purpose of the journey is no object but spiritual knowledge, a vision of the reality behind appearances, while the dreamer when he wakes can henceforth live his life on earth. The dreamer is,

theoretically, everyman; i.e., it is not by any act or virtue of his that he attains this vision, for the vision is a gift of Divine Grace. It does not necessarily follow that the vision will change his life, but if he does not change, his responsibility is greater than that of those who have never been granted his vision.[50]

In "The Seven Stages," the characters speak to each other, they describe what they experience, but they do not share a common vision, even though they advance from their four starting points into the same setting, a valley and then a steep pass through mountains (p. 63).[51] As they move through this collective psychic landscape, they split into pairs. First, Rosetta/Feeling and Emble/Sensation (youth with youth) move together away from Quant/Intuition and Malin/Thinking (age with age), and these pairs advance down through maritime plains to rival ports, to opposing harbors. Then they move inland and all come together again in a city. They find a house, Grandmother's House presumably, and when Rosetta steps inside, she immediately regrets looking out through the window at the Fallen World. Warned of the sadness of this vision, they run away from the place, each in his or her "rival nature," and come to a graveyard. Thoughts of death divide and link them a second time: Quant/Intuition goes with Rosetta/Feeling, and Emble/Sensation with Malin/Thinking. They come together again at the *hortus conclusus* common in medieval dream visions. Here, there are enclosed hermetic gardens "from the age of cypresses and cisterns."[52] Oddly, the wanderers experience the charm of this place as an accusation; like Adam and Eve, suddenly self-conscious as God walked through Eden in the cool of the evening, they feel ashamed. Each slips away alone into a labyrinth of dark forest and then from there into a desert.[53] When they eventually find each other again, they must face the individual and shared failure of this, their second exercise. The narrative ends with them waking up to where they sit in the bar on Third Avenue, and to who they are, together but alone. The narrator observes,

Their fears are confirmed, their hopes denied. For the world from which their journey has been one long flight rises up before them now as if the whole time it had been hiding in ambush, only waiting for the worst moment to reappear to its fugitives in all the majesty of its perpetual fury." (p. 96)

Their quest for "that state of prehistoric happiness" has failed, and they feel the worse for it.

Jacobs says it is "noteworthy" that Rosetta/Feeling and Malin/ Thinking never travel together, but he doesn't state why.[54] Curiously, he doesn't remark that neither do Emble/Sensation and Quant/Intuition ever explore their surroundings together. But Auden would have known why this should be so. Jung would position Rosetta and Malin as opposites on a rational axis, and Emble and Quant as opposites on an irrational axis, and in this schema, opposites are least likely to move together in the same direction. Jung writes,

> Feeling can never act as the secondary function alongside thinking, because it is by its very nature too strongly opposed to thinking. ... Thinking as a primary function can readily pair with intuition as the auxiliary, or indeed equally well with sensation, but, as already observed, never with feeling. Neither intuition nor sensation is antagonistic to thinking; they need not be absolutely excluded, for they are not of a nature equal to and opposite to thinking, as feeling is—which, as a judging function, successfully competes with thinking—but are functions of perception, affording welcome assistance to thinking.[55]

It is much more likely that a rational function and an irrational function may appear to align, traveling side by side, as they do in Auden's poem, on foot, by car, by rail or plane, on bicycles and boats. It is also more likely that functions on the same axis will feel oppositional, contradictory, producing what feel like impasses.[56] But when the four protagonists step out of the narrative structure of the dream and into a psychological state of disenchantment, they wake up, as it were, to Freud's reality principle.

The movement in search of "hope and health," imaged as nostalgically seeking home or regressively going back to the sealed garden, has failed. Now, in the third section, "The Dirge," the four protagonists leave the bar and take a taxi through the night streets of New York to Rosetta's Upper West Side apartment for a nightcap. The companions lament together in one voice, "Sob, heavy world, / Sob as you spin." They grieve, not for the failure of their regressive enterprise into a mythic past, but for the lost collective myth of the promising hero—"some semi-divine stranger with superhuman powers, some Gilgamesh or Napoleon"—who might rescue them from anguish and solitariness and chaos. In the context of the Second World War, if, as Jung hypothesized, France functioned as the unconscious of Germany, then Napoleon here is a precursor of Hitler (loath as the French still may be to admit to this).[57] Early twentieth-century fascism, with its promises of unity and ordered utopias through the exercise of radical authoritarian nationalism, contaminated any political interest in hero narratives and mythology. Jung acknowledged having slipped up badly in this regard, asking in a politically naïve way if there existed a positive potential in National Socialism through its connection to the myth of Wotan.[58]

In "The Dirge" the four protagonists grieve; in the next section, "The Masque," they compensate defensively. A masque is an entertainment in which masked players sing and dance; at the end, conventionally, the performers remove their masks and reveal their identities. Auden's protagonists mask themselves with manic artifice partly out of vanity, out of "the fear of getting too old to have fun or too ugly to get it," and partly out of unselfishness, not wanting to spoil things for the others. In Rosetta's apartment, they turn on a radio, not for news but for "Music past midnight," and Emble and Rosetta dance. A tiny spark of attraction has passed between them, and the narrator observes that "in times of war even the crudest kind of positive affection between persons seems extraordinarily beautiful" (p. 111). Quant and Malin half-hope that a spark of Eros has ignited between the youngsters; at the same time, they feel envious because it excludes them. Rosetta felt the erotic possibility with Emble back at the bar, invited everyone back to her flat, but was secretly disappointed when Quant and Malin accepted. Now Malin builds a little mock altar out of sandwiches and spills a libation onto the carpet; clearly the setting is profane, and neither Aphrodite nor Eros will drop, like a deus ex machina, into such a space. Rosetta and Emble tease each other with a mock marriage hymn, but their version of an Epithalamion to Hymen sounds like bad Cole Porter: "When you're depressed, I'll play the piano. / If you sigh, I'll sack cities." When Quant and Malin signal their readiness to leave, Rosetta sees them to the door and returns to find Emble passed out on her bed.

The Masque concludes with Rosetta's unmasking, with a great moving soliloquy. Her monologue, spoken to the hollow erotic space created by Emble's contradictory presence and absence on her bed, builds into a deeply expressed insight into her dilemma as a lover, as a woman, and also as a Jew who can no longer flee from the presence of God. She speaks as Feeling having to accept subjugation to the Self, to endure the subjective requiredness that Auden wrote about in his essay, "Perfectly Subjective":

> I wake into my existence to find myself and the world that is not
> myself already there, and simultaneously feel responsible for my
> discovery. I can and must ask: 'Who am I? Do I want to be? Who
> do I want and who ought I to become?' I am, in fact, an anxious
> subject. That is my religious problem. I experience subjective
> requiredness, i.e., a requiredness the source of which I cannot
> identify with anything I can call an object, and which concerns
> the meaning and value of my existence to myself. That is my
> immediate religious experience which allows me no rest until I
> believe I have understood it.[59]

She resigns herself to a life as one of God's subjects; she is subject
to God. God's covenant with her people, God's omnipresence, is both
her assurance and the cause of her anxiety because she cannot evade
"His Eye." His Law grants her no home, no patriarchal hero to affirm
the future, and no lover with whom to contradict her solitude.

In 1945, Auden had witnessed the devastation in Germany and
the hospitalization of survivors of the death camps. Jacobs points to
The Age of Anxiety as the first published poem in English to register
the fact of the Nazis' genocide; Rosetta says, "When bruised or
broiled our bodies are chucked / Like cracked crocks onto kitchen
middens" (p. 125).[60] Evoking the terrible solitary faith of Moses who
is permitted to see the back of God, Rosetta asks, "Who'll be left to
see it / Disconcerted? I'll be dumb before / The barracks burn and
boisterous Pharaoh / grow ashamed and shy" (p. 127). At the end of
the Masque, Rosetta manifests like the figure of Mrs. Avery with a
sword, guarding the gates of Eden in *Journey to a War*. Whatever
psychological ground has been traversed in *The Age of Anxiety*,
Rosetta's monologue declares there is no longer any recourse to going
back: "Though I fly to Wall Street / Or Publisher's Row, or pass out,
or / Submerge in music, or marry well, / Marooned in riches, He'll be
right there / With His eye upon me" (p. 125).

The poem concludes with the Epilogue, in which Quant and Malin
immediately separate, one going east, the other south. Quant trips
awkwardly up the stairs into his apartment and into the much-sought
oblivion of sleep. Malin, pondering alone, judges his own thinking as
"negative knowledge." In this secondary soliloquy closing Auden's
poem, the quality of thinking shifts from a negative philosophical to
a religious vocabulary: "Our minds insist on / Their own disorder as
their own punishment," but "His Truth makes our theories historical
sins." Malin finds potentiality in intellectually choosing the non-

intellectual religious perspective, in repenting his lack of faith in the Eternal that, made manifest in the now, could contradict "mad unbelief" with "mercy": "It is where we are wounded that is when He speaks / Our creaturely cry" (pp. 137–38). Rosetta and Malin both shift the ending of the poem by altering the rhetoric of anxiety; it remains a language without confidence or trust, without answers, but their words evoke something deeper and more anxiously hopeful than anything else in the poem.

Jacobs categorizes Auden's poem as "psychological" or "psycho-historical" and argues that the four protagonists are more "individual" by the end of the poem.[61] He refers to an essay in which Auden defines "individual" in two senses: "In the realm of nature, 'individual' means *to be something that others are not, to have uniqueness*: in the realm of spirit, it means *to become what one wills, to have a self-determined history.*"[62] Jacobs concludes that "no careful reader of the poem will be content to see any of them as simply a Jungian type." But Jacobs's reading of Jung is shallower than Auden's. It's correct that in good typological work, the type becomes more exacting, more precise in its functioning, but it is ego consciousness alone that becomes less identified with a Jungian type and more "individual" as it integrates the insights of the different functions.[63]

A distinction from the Jungian theory of dream interpretation might account for the problem with Jacobs's psychological interpretation, by calling it *objective* as opposed to *subjective*. For Jung, an objective interpretation of a dream links the significance of a dream interpersonally to people of vital importance in the outer life of the dreamer.[64] A subjective interpretation conceives all the dream figures as intrapsychic, personified features of the dreamer's personality. In good dream work, it's useful to consider both interpretations and ask if the dream better depicts an interpersonal situation with which the dreamer must grapple in outer reality or an intrapsychic one in which the figures in the dream are not important to the dreamer in outer reality. As a literary critic, Jacobs interprets the four personifications of types in *The Age of Anxiety* objectively, as if their significance resides in their individual personalities and their psychological progress as people. But a subjective, or "intrapsychic," reading of Auden's poem fits more convincingly. In this case, contrary to Jacobs's "objective interpretation," the careful reader sees that the four personified characters become increasingly delineated and precise but always as Jungian types. Individuation as a psychological process would be reflected in the narrative structure and the outcome of the poem as a whole.

Fuller inclines this way when he characterizes the work as Auden's attempt to represent subjectively "the four faculties of the fragmented psyche by four different characters."[65] Fuller also sets up a parallel with Kierkegaard's *Stadier paa Livensvegt* (*Stages on Life's Way*), in which invented characters (such as Johannes the Seducer and Victor Eremita) embody aspects of Kierkegaard himself. Auden showed that the four speakers are aspects of one psyche in a physical way, too—he insisted on controlling the design of the first edition of *The Age of Anxiety*.

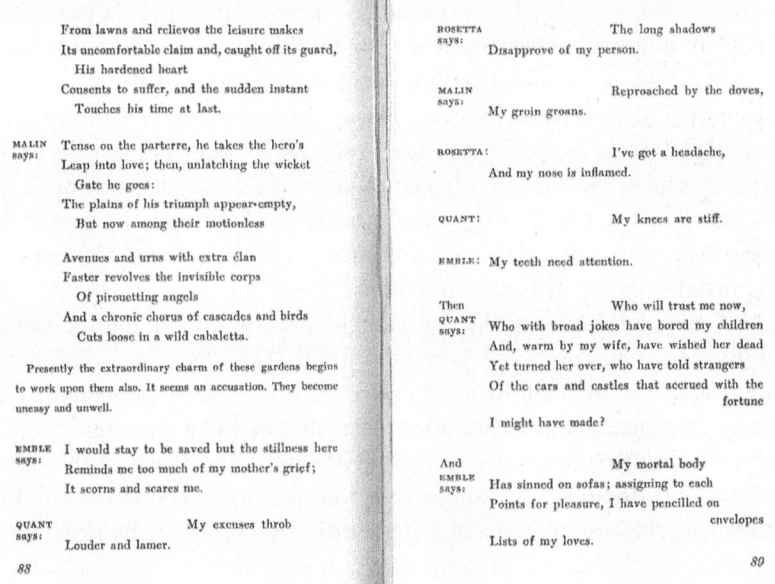

Figure 4: Auden's formatting design for The Age of Anxiety, Random House, 1947, author's collection.

The speakers' names are flush left, in their own column; they are signposts for the reader, but they are not part of the formal scheme of the poem itself. The narrator's words are set across both columns, flush left and justified across the page, in the style of prose.[66] This design supports a subjective interpretation of the poem as the intrapsychic braiding of four types of psychological functioning within one consciousness.[67] Susannah Young-ah Gottlieb emphasizes the paradox of this plurality of four perspectives that is also a uniformity conveyed by a singular verse style: "Any attempt to grasp the poem requires, therefore, a poetics that is rich enough to encompass this apparent contradiction between the uniformity of the poetic line and the development and envelopment of a plurality of perspectives in the course of the poem."[68] And she identifies the single, dominant affect of these four shifting humors as "the anxiety of individuation."[69]

In the end, Feeling speaks a monologue with as much heft as the monologue spoken by Thinking. The psychological space defined by the poem in a linear narrative sequence privileges Thinking and Intuition—they are the first and also the last to speak, and Thinking functions as the guide to the first movement, "The Seven Ages." But Intuition invites Feeling to function as guide to the dream-quest in "The Seven Stages," and Feeling travels (and momentarily flirts) with Sensation and also travels with Intuition. At the end Feeling has the longest speech in the poem, with an authority equal to but different from that of Thinking: feminine to masculine, but more importantly, metaphorically lunar to solar. Both Feeling and Thinking (as opposite functions that Jung locates on a rational axis) address the problem of anxiety in wartime as disordering. Both transpose that anxiety—the loss of recourse to images of being at home in the world in the past or the future and the loss of the solace of connecting with others in the moment, of *communitas*—into a religious problem that must be suffered, a purgatorial experience endured in the omnipresence of the Self. Rosetta as Feeling speaks of "anxious hope" and also of integrity, of a Oneness; her last words are, in Hebrew, the Jewish credo, *"Sh'ma Yisrael / Adonai eloheinu, adonai echad"* (Hear, O Israel, the Lord our God, the Lord is one).

A theory of psychological types and a list of conventional narrative forms are both taxonomies, heuristic ways of classifying human experience and discerning the world. Jung constructed a theory in order to view the psyche as a totality, and, at the same time, he qualified his theory in order to avoid totalizing. "No one, I trust, will draw the conclusion from my description of types that I believe the four or eight types here presented to be the only ones that exist," he says in *Psychological Types*. "This would be a serious misconception, for I have no doubt whatever that these attitudes could also be considered and classified from other points of view."[70] I said earlier that Auden, as an Introverted Thinking type, began by choosing a narrative form and then discovering intuitively what started to emerge from within that form as soon as he had defined it, and he called *The Age of Anxiety* a "baroque eclogue." An eclogue is a narrative form that adopts the pastoral convention in which a natural setting is contrasted with an artificial style of diction. In an eclogue, traditionally, lowly shepherds exchange ideas in high-toned debate. Generally, the term *baroque* means highly ornamented, but Auden defined the Baroque more politically as "the counter-reformation's theatrical use of matter against the abstract and earnest thinking of the Reformers."[71] On the title page itself, then, Auden signals to readers that they are about to step into a self-conscious narrative, a highly ornate artificial construct in which they will find a sharp contrast between the ordinariness of the setting, the bar on Third Avenue, and the heightened language of the speakers: a theatrical use of matter against thinking. Auden's adaptation of medieval alliterative verse, the form of his beloved *Piers Plowman*, is also a highly formalized choice for a modern American poem. Jacobs complains that, as a result, the poem is off-putting, even inaccessible, and judged a failure, perhaps reading his and other critics' own limitations onto the poem. In fact, the strict form and style of *The Age of Anxiety* function, in part, to contain the breadth of the turmoil and the depth of the dread that emerge when anxiety breaks through into consciousness. The challenging psychology of Auden's literary work addresses the question of how individual and collective anxiety can be expressed meaningfully; the answer suggests, in part, that its expression comes in heightened waves and that it must be very formally contained.[72]

The epigraph of *The Age of Anxiety* is also formal: "*Lacrimosa dies illa / Qua resurget ex favilla / Judicandus homo reus.*" Auden quotes from the ancient poem *Dies Irae*, "Day of Wrath," the most famous hymn for All Souls Day. "Lacrimosa," its eighteenth and penultimate stanza, begins: "Ah, that day of tears and mourning, / From the dust of earth returning, / Man for judgement must prepare him."[73] Auden employs it as a signpost, and it situates readers from the start in a Dantean cosmology and in an ascending purgatorial state. Fuller, always helpful, notes that at the time, Auden was reading Eugen Rosenstock-Huessy's *Out of Revolution: Autobiography of Western Man* (1938) and expressed interest in the celebration of All Souls Day as instituted by the Catholic Church in AD 998. For Auden, the culmination of human history signified by the Last Judgment conveyed more than terror; it emphasized human dignity, in that humankind rises up, individual by individual, claiming "not to be thrown into the fire like a weed, but to be judged."[74] This differentiation between anxiety and terror will bring us to consider not so much how *The Age of Anxiety* was composed and read in 1947 but more how we read it in our time, which I will address in Chapter 4.

The last words of the poem Auden gives not to any of the four functions but to his narrator, who describes stepping with the reader out of the sacred temenos of the poem and back into the profane world "where time is real and in which, therefore, poetry can take no interest" (p. 138).

NOTES

1. "He is an extremely novel and original poet, but at the same time has extraordinary gifts of imitation, of mimicry, of taking and making his own. He is unusually skilful at analysing someone else's work, taking out what he likes, and synthesizing a new style of his own that will include this." Randall Jarrell, *Randall Jarrell on W. H. Auden*, ed. Stephen Burt (New York: Colombia University Press, 2005), pp. 20–1.

2. "The three greatest influences on my own work have been, I think, Dante, Langland, and Pope." W. H. Auden, "Criticism in a Mass Society," *The Intent of the Critic*, ed. Donald Stauffer, 1941, in *The Collected Works of W. H. Auden*, prose, vol. 2, ed. Edward Mendelson (Princeton, NJ: Princeton University Press, 2002), p. 92.

3. Fuller emphasizes that Auden was "in a Jungian frame of mind" in the years 1939–1945. John Fuller, *W. H. Auden: A Commentary* (London: Faber and Faber, 1998), p. 311.

4. See W. H. Auden, *Juvenilia: Poems, 1922–1928*, ed. Katherine Bucknell (Princeton, NJ: Princeton University Press, 1994), p. 232; with regard to Auden's composition of this 1927 poem, Fuller cites Jung's *Modern Man in Search of a Soul* (1933), but it should be noted that *Psychological Types* had already appeared in 1923 in an English translation by H. G. Baynes, with the subtitle, *The Psychology of Individuation* (published by Kegan Paul); and a short essay on "Psychological Types," translated by H. G. and Cary F. Baynes, appeared in *Contributions to Analytical Psychology* (London, 1928).

5. W. H. Auden, "Family Ghosts," *Collected Poems* (London: Faber and Faber, 1976/1991), pp. 40–1. As mentioned in Chapter 1, Auden's dramatic poem *Paid on Both Sides* (1928) depicts the antagonism between the Nowers and the Shaws as intergenerationally transmitted. Fuller points out that Auden could also have acquired this notion from Homer Lane, as edited by Layard: "All organic life may be represented as a wish. Man, the highest form of life, is himself the product of the cumulative wishes of all organic life in past ages." Homer Lane, *Talks to Parents and Teachers*, 1928, p. 177, in Fuller, *W. H. Auden*, p. 80.

6. W. H. Auden, "Psychology and Art Today," *The Arts Today*, ed. Geoffrey Grigson, 1935, in Auden, *Collected Works*, vol. 1, pp. 93–105.

7. W. H. Auden, Sonnet XXI, "In Time of War," *Journey to a War*, in Auden, *Collected Works*, vol. 1, p. 677.

8. W. H. Auden, "In Memory of Ernst Toller," *The New Yorker*, Jun. 17, 1939, in *Collected Poems*, pp. 249–50.

9. Fuller, *W. H. Auden*, p. 290.

10. W. H. Auden, "Jacob and the Angel," Review of *Behold, This Dreamer!* by Walter de la Mare, Dec. 27, 1939, in Auden, *Collected Works*, vol. 2, p. 37.

11. Edward Mendelson evaluates Auden's review as "a lurid archetypal parable ... written in an exalted visionary tone." See Edward Mendelson, *Later Auden* (New York: Farrar Straus and Giroux, 1999), p. 91; in his more recent introduction, he describes it as "stylistically heightened prose." Edward Mendelson, "Introduction," in Auden, *Collected Works*, vol. 2, p. xviii; for the Jung essay, see "The Phenomenology of the Spirit in Fairy Tales," *The Archetypes and the Collective Unconscious*, in *The Collected Works of C. G Jung*, vol. 7, ed. and trans. Gerhard Adler and R. F. C. Hull (Princeton, NJ: Princeton University Press; 1969), §§ 207–54.

12. W. H. Auden, letter to John Layard, quoted in Mendelson, *Later Auden*, p. 95.

13. W. H. Auden, "Eros and Agape," a review of *Love in the Western World* by Denis de Rougemont, in Auden, *Collected Works*, vol. 2, p. 140.

14. W. H. Auden, "Opera on an American Legend," *The New York Times*, May 4, 1941, in Auden, *Collected Works*, vol. 2, p. 129.

15. Fuller, *W. H. Auden*, p. 313.

16. W. H. Auden, *The Sea and the Mirror: A Commentary on Shakespeare's The Tempest*, ed. Arthur Kirsch (Princeton, NJ: Princeton University Press, 2003); Alan Jacobs notes that in 1963 Auden wrote in the margin of a copy of *For the Time Being*: "Bosh, straight from Jung." It's not clear if this marginal note indicates that Auden came to reject Jung's ideas outright or if he repudiated himself for not making the ideas work poetically in the oratorio. See Alan Jacobs, "Introduction," in W. H. Auden, *The Age of Anxiety*, ed. Alan Jacobs (Princeton, NJ: Princeton University Press, 2011), p. xx.

17. Humphrey Carpenter, *W. H. Auden: A Biography* (Boston, MA: Houghton Mifflin, 1981), p. 19; for a scathing assessment of the systemic abuse inherent to the English boarding school experience, see Joy Schaverien, "Boarding School: The Trauma of the 'Privileged' Child," *Journal of Analytical Psychology* 49 (5, 2004): 683–705.

18. W. H. Auden, "Poet and Politician," *Common Sense*, January 1940, in Auden, *Collected Works*, vol. 2, p. 41.

19. W. H. Auden, "A Literary Transference," *Southern Review*, Summer 1940, in Auden, *Collected Works*, vol. 2, p. 44.

20. W. H. Auden, Introduction to *Tales of Grimms and Anderson*, December 1947, published 1952, in Auden, *Collected Works*, vol. 2, p. 392.

21. W. H. Auden, *Forewords & Afterwords* (New York: Vintage, 1997), p. 502.

22. W. H. Auden, *The Dyer's Hand* (London: Faber and Faber, 1963), p. 34.

23. W. H. Auden, *The English Auden*, p. 398, in Carpenter, *W. H. Auden*, pp. 14–5.

24. Carpenter, *W. H. Auden*, p. 31.

25. Alan Ansen, *The Table Talk of W. H. Auden*, ed. Nicholas Jenkins (Princeton, NJ: Ontario Review Press, 1990), p. 19.

26. W. H. Auden, letter to Stephen Spender, Autumn 1940, in Carpenter, *W. H. Auden*, p. 31; Stephen Spender, *World Within World* (New York: Modern Library, 1951/2001), pp. 59–62. In his autobiography, Stephen Spender wrote this assessment of the Auden he first encountered at Oxford:

> His clinical view of living, whereby he regarded life as an operation performed by a surgically minded individual upon the carefully analysed and examined body and soul of the

society round him, was amoral. He rejected, quietly and without fuss, the moral views of both his preceptors and his fellow undergraduates. The only generally accepted virtue which he himself accepted was courage: because courage was required by anyone wishing to achieve his own independent development. ... Auden, despite his perceptiveness, lacked something in human relationships. He forced issues too much, made everyone too conscious of himself and therefore was in the position of an observer who is a disturbing force in the behaviour he observes. Sometimes he gave the impression of playing an intellectual game with himself and with others, and this meant that in the long run he was rather isolated. His early poetry also gives the impression of an intellectual game—a game to which the name Clinical Detachment might be given. It is a game of impartial objectivity about catastrophes, wars, revolutions, violence, hatred, loves, and all the forces which move through human lives. But this attitude of the young poet with a bird's-eye view on human calamity in a world of wars and dismantled works runs the risk of becoming facilely inhuman. Auden himself was too human, moreover, for it to be an attitude which he could for long maintain in the face of experiences that wrung his heart. After all, the young poet does become involved, he cannot regard justice and injustice, love and hatred, life and death, with exactly the same impartiality, tracing them with icy precision, like the features of a frozen landscape. But although Auden ceased to be detached, joined movements, wrote love poetry, accepted the Anglican creed, I am not sure whether he completely broke away from the isolation in human relationships which was simply the result of his overwhelming cleverness as a young man. ... But if Auden's answers, which have been psychoanalysis, political revolution, universal love and Christian dogma, have never quite lost their arbitrary, experimental quality, as though they were repeated attempts to understand the nature of a problem, and to solve it by the arrangement of its elements according to certain hypotheses, nevertheless the problem itself is ever more profoundly understood and brilliantly illustrated. And the problem is Man in this Century. Auden is certainly an intellectual poet: but to say this in a way which would imply that he has only an intellectual grasp of things would be to underestimate him. He has an intellectual understanding of situations which he states with his heart as well as his intellect, and if the solution which he offers to the problem seems intellectualized the problem itself is completely realized.

27. Mendelson, *Later Auden*, pp. 194–97.

28. This scoutmaster reference may allude to Orwell's early criticism of Auden as a "gutless Kipling" writing poetry of boy-scout

"uplift" (See Chapter 1, p.13). That is to say, the negative inner critic in Auden employed Orwell's diction.

29. Dorothy Farnan, *Auden in Love* (New York: Plume, 1985), p. 27. Farnan notes that "Sid" refers to Chester Kallman's first stepmother, Syd Herman Kallman, whom Chester detested, and that Elsie was a Brooklyn friend.

30. W. H. Auden, "To Chester Kallman, b. Jan. 7, 1921," in Farnan, *Auden in Love*, pp. 25–7.

31. Mendelson, *Later Auden*, pp. 175–76.

32. W. H. Auden, "Romantic or Free," *Smith Alumnae Quarterly*, August 1940, in Auden, *Collected Works*, vol. 2, p. 69.

33. W. H. Auden, "Lecture Notes," *The Commonweal*, Nov. 6, 1942, in Auden, *Collected Works*, vol. 2, p. 162.

34. Jacobs, "Introduction," p. xviii.

35. Søren Kierkegaard, *The Concept of Anxiety: A Simple Psychologically Oriented Deliberation in View of the Dogmatic Problem of Hereditary Sin*, trans. Alastair Hannay (New York: Liveright Publishing, 2014).

36. W. H. Auden, "A Preface to Kierkegaard" (1944), in Auden, *Collected Works*, vol. 2, p. 214.

37. Another example of Auden's ruthless honesty with himself as a poet and a lover was the line "Thousands have lived without love, not one without water" in "First Things First" (1957), in Auden, *Collected Poems*, p. 584. Nicholas Jenkins writes,

> Auden once claimed that the 'nicest poetic compliment' he ever received came in 1957 when his friend the Catholic activist Dorothy Day was arrested and held at what was then called the "House of Detention for Women" at the corner of 6th Avenue and West 10th Street in Manhattan. She told him that as the women prisoners were marched down for their weekly shower, a prostitute recited this line from Auden's poem, which had recently appeared in *The New Yorker*. Auden commented, not wholly ironically, 'I knew I hadn't written in vain!'

See Nicholas Jenkins, "Historical as Munich—Auden at 100: Who Is He Now?" *Times Literary Supplement*, Feb. 9, 2007, pp. 13–4.

38. W. H. Auden, *New Republic*, May 15, 1944, in Auden, *Collected Works*, vol. 2, p. 214.

39. Jung employs the Greek word *temenos* to demarcate a piece of land, to describe making a "safe space" where mental work can take

place. A temenos is where an encounter with the unconscious can be had and where personified unconscious contents can safely be brought into the light of consciousness. See C. G. Jung, *Psychology and Alchemy*, in *The Collected Works of C. G. Jung*, vol. 12, ed. and trans. Gerhard Adler and R. F. C. Hull (Princeton, NJ: Princeton University Press, 1953/1968), § 63.

40. C. G. Jung, "The Therapeutic Value of Abreaction" (1928), *The Practice of Psychotherapy*, in *The Collected Works of C. G. Jung*, vol. 16, ed. and trans. Gerhard Adler and R. F. C. Hull (Princeton, NJ: Princeton University Press, 1954), §§ 129–38.

41. W. H. Auden, letter to John Pudney, April 1931 (Berg Collection), in Carpenter, *W. H. Auden*, p. 55.

42. "Now Our Endless Journey Stops": W. H. Auden and the Time of the Incarnation, ABC Religions and Ethics, Australian Broadcasting Corporation, Jan. 3, 2014. p. 2; and Alan Jacobs, "Introduction," in W. H. Auden, *For the Time Being*, ed. Alan Jacobs (Princeton, NJ: Princeton University Press, 2013). Jacobs writes, "A kind of *psychomachia* or internal warfare is the common lot of humanity, a point Auden develops in *The Age of Anxiety*."

43. Jung writes,

> The four functions are somewhat like the four points of a compass; they are just as arbitrary and just as indispensable. Nothing prevents our shifting the cardinal points as many degrees as we like in one direction or the other, or giving them different names. It is merely a question of convention and intelligibility. But one thing I must confess: I would not for anything dispense with this compass on my psychological voyages of discovery. This is not merely for the obvious, all-too-human reason that everyone is in love with his own ideas. I value the type theory for the objective reason that it provides a system of comparison and orientation which makes possible something that has long been lacking, a critical psychology.

See C. G. Jung, "A Psychological Theory of Types" (1931), in *Modern Man In Search of a Soul*, trans. W. S. Dell and Cary F. Baynes (London: Routledge and Kegan Paul, 1933); Reprinted in appendix to C. G. Jung, *Psychological Types*, in *The Collected Works of C. G. Jung*, vol. 6, ed. and trans. Gerhard Adler and R. F. C. Hull (Princeton, NJ: Princeton University Press, 1971), §§ 958–59; and Kristine Arnet Connidis emphasizes the uses of Jung's typology as a "compass" and his creation of a "critical psychology," and she innovatively applies Jung's types to the field of law in K. A. Connidis, "Court and Government in Conflict: Judicial and Political Decision-making from a Critical Psychology Perspective" (unpublished Ph.D. diss., University of Toronto, 2015).

44. Auden made a private list of the romantic relationships that changed his life: (1) Robert Medley; (2) Christopher Isherwood; (3) Michael Yates, the subject of "Lay Your Sleeping Head, My Love"; (4) Chester Kallman; and (5) Rhoda Jaffe.

45. Edward Callan, "Allegory in Auden's *The Age of Anxiety*," *Twentieth Century Literature* 10.4 (1965): 155–65.

46. All quotations from the poem are from W. H. Auden, *The Age of Anxiety* (New York: Random House, 1946/1947).

47. Shakespeare, *As You Like It*, 2.7.138–65. References are to act, scene, and line.

48. Jacobs emphasizes that Auden's characterizations are not intended to be novelistic but rather resemble those of a taxonomic psychologist, and he tracks this heuristic tradition back through Prudentius's *Psychomachia* to Theophrastus's *Moral Characters*; see Jacobs, "Introduction" in Auden, *The Age of Anxiety*, pp. xxvii-xxviii. Likewise, in *Psychological Types*, Jung examines the problem of types from classical and medieval traditions through Schiller, Goethe, and the philosophy of William James before introducing his own model.

49. Jung also knew Francesco Colonna's *Hypnerotomachia Poliphili, ubi humana omnia non nisi somnium esse docet (The Strife of Love in a Dream)*, through Linda Fierz-David's published commentary, for which Jung wrote a preface. In this allegorical and mythological romance attributed to Francesco Colonna, first published in Venice by Aldus Manutius, 1499, Poliphilo ("friend of many things") pursues his love Polia ("many things") through a dreamlike landscape and is seemingly at least reconciled with her by the Fountain of Venus. For the only translation into English of the entire text, see Francesco Colonna, *Hypnerotomachia Poliphili: The Strife of Love in a Dream*, trans. Joscelyn Godwin (New York: Thames and Hudson, 1999); see C. G. Jung, "Foreword to Fierz-David: *The Dream of Poliphilo*" (1946), in *The Symbolic Life*, in *The Collected Works of C. G. Jung*, vol. 19, ed. and trans. Gerhard Adler and R. F. C. Hull (Princeton, NJ: Princeton University Press, 1961), §§ 780–81.

50. W. H. Auden, "K's Quest," in *The Kafka Problem*, ed. Angel Flores (1946), in Auden, *Collected Works*, vol. 2, p. 283.

51. Auden notes that the landscape in the Stages corresponds to the human body; in the *Zohar*, the spirits travel through the body, taking leave of each part, and then each part dies. Auden mapped the body beginning with the belly, the breasts, the heart, the hands as rival ports, the throat, the brain as house, the forehead complex as graveyard, the back as the desert. See Fuller, *W. H. Auden*, p. 379.

52. Alan Jacobs helpfully points here to *Hortulus Hermeticus* ("The Hermetic Garden"), an emblem book published in 1627 by the alchemist Daniel Stolz von Stolzenberg. Jacobs, in Auden, *Age of Anxiety*, p. 134, n. 69.

53. Susan Young-ah Gottlieb takes up Auden's clue about mapping the landscape of the Seven Stages on the *Zohar*'s symbolic reading of the human body, and she brilliantly argues that the desert, the last setting before the four emerge from this dream narrative, is the back: "for the *Zohar* repeatedly refers to the theophantic moment *par excellence*—the moment when Moses, while crossing through a desert that will prepare his people for a promised land of cypresses and cisterns, is allowed to see God's back (Exodus 33: 21–2)." Susannah Young-ah Gottlieb, *Regions of Sorrow: Anxiety and Messianism in Hannah Arendt and W. H. Auden* (Stanford, CA: Stanford University Press, 2003), p. 109.

54. Jacobs, "Introduction," in Auden, *Age of Anxiety*, p. xxx.

55. Jung, *Psychological Types*, CW 6, §§ 667–68.

56. Susannah Young-ah Gottlieb observes that "Rosetta may be seeking to oppose Malin in the most rigorous manner possible." Gottlieb, *Regions of Sorrow*, p. 101.

57. C. G. Jung said, "This is really a problem. I explain it to myself this way: The relationship between Germany and France is like conscious and unconscious. For the French, Germany is the country of the unconscious." See "Minutes to the Discussion of the 1945 Lecture," in *On Psychological and Visionary Art: Notes on Jung's Lecture on Nerval's "Aurélia,"* ed. Craig Stephenson (Princeton, NJ: Princeton University Press, 2015), p. 84.

58. Auden had just read Joseph Campbell and Henry Morton Robinson's *A Skeleton Key to Finnegans Wake* (1944) in which James Joyce's H. C. Earwicker is the "great progenitor" who manifests himself as Woden, Thor, St. Patrick, and Cromwell. Mendelson, *Later Auden*, p. 252; see also C. G. Jung, "Wotan: A Psychologist Explores the Forces Behind German Fascism," in *The Saturday Review of*

Literature (Oct. 16, 1937): 3–4, 19; and C. G. Jung, "Wotan" (1936), *Civilization in Transition*, in *The Collected Works of C. G. Jung*, vol. 10, ed. and trans. Gerhard Adler and R. F. C. Hull (Princeton, NJ: Princeton, 1964/1978), §§ 179–93.

59. W. H. Auden, "Purely Subjective," *The Chimera*, Summer 1943, in Auden, *Collected Works*, vol. 2, p. 184.

60. Jacobs, "Introduction," in Auden, *Age of Anxiety*, p. xiii.

61. *Ibid.*, p. xxxv.

62. W. H. Auden, "Introduction," in Charles Baudelaire, *Intimate Journals*, trans. Christopher Isherwood (1947), in Auden, *Collected Works*, vol. 2, p. 308.

63. See John Beebe, "Psychological Types," in *The Handbook of Jungian Psychology: Theory, Practice, and Applications*, ed. Renos Papadopoulos (Hove: Routledge, 2006), pp. 130–52; "Understanding consciousness through the theory of psychological types," in *Analytical Psychology: Contemporary Perspectives in Jungian Analysis*, ed. Joseph Cambray and Linda Carter (London: Brunner-Routledge, 2004), pp. 83–115; and *Energies and Patterns of Psychological Type: The Reservoir of Consciousness* (Hove: Routledge, 2016).

64. Jacob's "objective" reading also leads to his complaint that the book is not widely read and has never been fully understood; it fails because "the experiences of the characters here are abstract and intellectual to the highest degree." Jacobs even quotes Auden against himself: in writing about Kierkegaard, Auden observed, "a planetary visitor might read through the whole of his voluminous works without discovering that human beings are not ghosts but have bodies of flesh and blood." W. H. Auden, *Modern Canterbury Pilgrims*, in *The Collected Works of W. H. Auden*, prose, vol. 3, ed. Edward Mendelson (Princeton, NJ: Princeton University Press, 2002), p. 579; Jacobs lays the same charge against Auden.

For Jung on "objective" versus "subjective" dream interpretation, see C. G. Jung, "General Aspects of Dream Psychology," *The Structures and Dynamics of the Psyche*, in *The Collected Works of C. G. Jung*, vol. 8, ed. and trans. Gerhard Adler and R. F. C. Hull (Princeton, NJ: Princeton University Press, 1960/1981), §§ 509–10.

Glyn Maxwell made a similar complaint: "The four characters all sound the same. They are abstractions, and in their speeches, they don't show the faintest signs of attention to one another. They hardly ever respond to what another has said, "as if the four abstractions were true oppositions, or sealed off from each other like the four elements." Glyn Maxwell, "W. H. Auden's 'The Age of Anxiety,'" *The Guardian*, Apr. 10, 2010.

65. Fuller refers to Jung's *t'ai chi t'u*, a diagrammatic representation of the process of the psyche; see Jolande Jacobi, *The Psychology of C. G. Jung*, 6th ed., pp. 10ff.

66. Ansen, *Table Talk*, p. 21. I received as a gift a copy of *The Age of Anxiety* with Auden's original design. He chose a small, elegant Victorian typeface and devised a layout that emphasized the poem's "baroque" character:

> In my contract for *The Age of Anxiety*, I specified that I wanted to have control over the details of printing. Now they bow and scrape whenever I come into the office. They used to treat me like an unwelcome office boy. But I don't like all this kow-towing. The man in charge must be very annoyed over having to make a fuss over me since he must think I blame him for the things I don't like—and I do. The book is going to be very small, the poetry is set in very small type and the prose still smaller.

67. In an article on Skelton, Auden notes favorably that all the characters speak like the author. See Auden, *Collected Works*, vol. 1, p. 92. Even Mendelson points to the archaic metre as suggesting "the common archetypal depths beneath the individualizing surface of the urban psyche." Mendelson, *Later Auden*, pp. 243–45.

68. Gottlieb, *Regions of Sorrow*, p. 70.

69. *Ibid.*, p. 86.

70. Jung, *Psychological Types*, CW 6, § 848; and see C. G. Jung, "Foreword to the Argentine Edition," *Psychological Types*, CW 6, pp. xiv–xv. In 1934, Jung regretfully acknowledged:

> Indeed, even in medical circles the opinion has got about that my method of treatment consists in fitting patients into this system and giving them corresponding 'advice.' This regrettable misunderstanding completely ignores the fact that this kind of classification is nothing but a childish parlour game, every bit as futile as the division of mankind into brachycephalics and dolichocephalics. My typology is far rather a critical apparatus serving to sort out and organize the welter of empirical material, but not in any sense to stick labels on people at first sight. It is not a physiognomy and not an anthropological system, but a critical psychology dealing with the organization and delimitation of psychic processes that can be shown to be typical.

71. W. H. Auden, Swarthmore seminar in Romanticism, in Mendelson, *Later Auden*, p. 261.

72. In this regard, Auden observed, "I have come to feel that most Americans are profoundly lonely, and that in this more than in anything else lies the explanation of American violence." Auden, "Poet and Politician," p. 42.

73. English translation of "Lacrimosa," part of the *Dies Irae* sequence in the Requiem mass. *Dies Irae* by William Josiah Irons in 1849. Accessed Jun. 8, 2015, at http://en.wikipedia.org/wiki/Dies_Irae.

74. Fuller, *W. H. Auden*, p. 371; see also Jacobs in Auden, *Age of Anxiety*, p. 117, n. xxxi.

Figure 1: Auden and Leonard Bernstein, photograph by Ben Greenhaus, courtesy of New York Philharmonic Archives.

CHAPTER THREE

CREATIVE EXTRAPOLATIONS

Bernstein—Robbins—Neumeier—Scarlett

Auden finished *The Age of Anxiety* in early December 1946.[1] As I mentioned, the book won the Pulitzer Prize for poetry, but critical responses were polarized. On the one hand, in *Harper's Magazine*, Columbia professor and critic Jacques Barzun described the book as an essential reference for understanding the Zeitgeist of the war: "I have not the slightest doubt that when books analyzing our plight are read only by candidates for degrees, Auden's eclogue will be quoted, in bits, as a sufficient token of our times."[2] On the other hand, in the *Partisan Review*, the American poet Delmore Schwartz expressed puzzlement: "It is the most self-indulgent book Auden has written. ... The eloquent dialectic inherent in the use of dialogue comes to almost nothing because each character often speaks as if he had not heard what the previous character just said."[3] And when the book was published a little later in England, the critic Alan Ross, reviewing it in the *Times Literary Supplement*, wrote (in that English scoutmaster tone that Auden had worked so hard to expunge from his own voice): "Mr. Auden has written his one dull book, his one failure. Perhaps it may turn out to be the most salutary thing that has yet happened in an astonishing career."[4]

But the book's literary reception turned out to be less vital than the creative responses by other artists: Leonard Bernstein, Jerome Robbins, John Neumeier, and Liam Scarlett. Transmuting Auden's poetry into music and movement, these artists engaged, deliberately or unawares, with the taxonomy of types as they restated Auden's warning to compensate with dialectic during eristic times. Auden became their invisible bridge to Jung.

LEONARD BERNSTEIN, *THE AGE OF ANXIETY*: SYMPHONY NO. 2, 1949

On July 27, 1947, Richard Adams Romney wrote to his friend, the young composer and conductor Leonard Bernstein:

> This morning's book list from *Holiday* advertises Auden's new thing along with a new one of Edith Sitwell's. When I get round to send you [*The Age of*] *Anxiety* I will also include *The Shadow of Cain* which the book store insists 'reflects more directly the tragic impact of contemporary events on an acutely sensitive and perceptive nature.' And then they add, 'In their likeness and unlikeness, these two books are an absorbing study.'

Romney's letter closes: "Why don't you try a tone poem of *Anxiety*. The four themes—their inter-relationship, pairing-off drama, etc. might make a good thing."[5] Romney's reference here to "the four themes" refers to Jung's four psychological types.

Nigel Simeone, the editor of Bernstein's letters, does not include Bernstein's reply to Romney's suggestion (Was there a further letter or a telephone conversation?), but two days later, on July 29, 1947, Romney writes back, insisting that Bernstein transpose Auden's eclogue into music not for a ballet but for the concert hall. "What do you think of the *Anxiety* idea?," he asks.

> There is so much musical subtlety in it, and those various meters brought about by the different roads the couples take and their differing means of transportation, to say nothing of the moods, and the separateness that becomes oneness under alcohol and/ or libidinal urges. You mentioned it being good ballet material, yes, but I think, first, it should be composed as music by itself and therefore protect it from being too obvious program music, and then if some clever choreographer can put the musical composition to work, with what added quality good music may give to the themes and material, well and good. I would rather have 'it' in the concert hall, where it can be less 'handled' than in the ballet school where many talents brush it up. It's too good a thing for many hands.[6]

According to Romney, Bernstein should trust the poem's structure and the musicality inherent in Auden's diction.

Three years earlier, on July 26, 1944, Bernstein had sent his mentor, the conductor Serge Alexandrovich Koussevitzky, a birthday greeting and a gift of twenty-two bars of music: "Please accept this little sketch now, and let us hope it grows into a composition worthy of your greatness." Nigel Simeone emphasizes that the idea in the so-called "sketch" was remarkably fully formed.

Figure 2: Leonard Bernstein, birthday greeting and musical sketch to Serge Koussevitzky, July 26, 1944. Holograph. Courtesy of the Leonard Bernstein Office, Boosey and Hawkes, and the Library of Congress.

Now, responding to Romney's suggestion, Bernstein returned to this sketch and used it as his way into the task of reimagining Auden's words as music. Always searching for distinctively American musical idioms, Bernstein was delighted to discover that Auden had written *The Age of Anxiety* in American vernacular, with a good deal of wordplay.[7] Auden's manipulation of rhythm intrigued Bernstein; he saw the variety of meters within the six-part structure, and he noticed the ironic pastiches of popular songs and jazz riffs sung by the characters or heard over the radio in the bar and in Rosetta's apartment. Most important, Bernstein found at the end of the Masque the sudden avowal of Jewish faith voiced in Rosetta's monologue and, in the Epilogue, a correspondingly powerful visual image of Malin underground on a subway train, then emerging out of darkness onto the Manhattan bridge at dawn.

Bernstein understood immediately that Auden's characters are four psychological functions of one self at least partly because he had been in therapy himself with psychoanalyst Marketa Morris for five years. In Prague, Morris had given classes in child psychology to teachers from 1936 to 1938 before coming to North America and establishing a practice in New York City. In his letters to friends such as Aaron Copland, Bernstein refers to her a little patronizingly as "the Frau," but he acknowledges her insightfulness and confesses his hope for a positive psychotherapeutic outcome. For her part, the letters to him suggest that, because of Bernstein's relentless travel schedule, she feels frustrated about the quality of the therapeutic frame and the effectiveness of their analytic work.[8] They ended their sessions late in 1947.

After 1948, Bernstein gained even more familiarity with the notion of psychological types while working with Jungian analyst Renée Noll.[9] In 1938 Noll had escaped from Nazi Berlin to Switzerland, where she had studied with Jung. A pioneer in work with young offenders, she had also established the Country Place in Litchfield, Connecticut, as "a residential community for the psychologically disturbed adult who has more insight than he or she can use, who knows how he or she should act but withdraws from action." In his work with Noll, Bernstein came to differentiate between his personal narcissism and his creativity as an artist, attempting to privilege the latter over the former:

I can begin really to live my life (as I can now) and not only live on the circumference of it. And, willy-nilly, Renée has helped to that point—a point where my world changes from one of abstractions and public-hungry performance to one of reality, a world of creativity.[10]

At the same time, Bernstein complained about his overly mother-son therapeutic alliance with Noll, which he characterized as too permissive or lenient: "My feeling is one totally apart from analysis; I want only to cope, and through my own powers, without aid—especially of the indulgent, personal sort that was forthcoming from Miss Nell."[11] (Psychoanalysts would note the opposites constellated in the transferences manifested between Bernstein and Morris, the too-stern parent, and Noll, the too-permissive.) By 1950, Bernstein terminated the analytic work with Noll.

Just as important as the influence of these psychoanalysts was an event in Bernstein's life in the summer of 1948. Bernstein seized the opportunity to drive across America, from Tanglewood, New York, to Taos, New Mexico, in the company of his younger brother Burton and the English poet Stephen Spender.[12] A close friend of Auden's, Spender had just finished teaching a semester at Sarah Lawrence College, and he had accepted Frieda Lawrence's invitation to stay at D. H. Lawrence's high mountain ranch, 6500 feet above Taos, in order to write his autobiography, *World Within World* (1949).[13] Bernstein would have discussed Auden's life and work with Spender and also heard Spender hold forth on the significance of the interior life. Bernstein then profited from the seclusion at Taos in his attempts to complete the second symphony.

Bernstein might have called his Second Symphony a piano concerto, although he rejected that description. He wrote,

I imagine that the conception of a symphony with piano solo emerges from the personal identification of myself with the poem. In this sense, the pianist provides an autobiographical protagonist, set against an orchestral mirror in which he sees himself, analytically, in the modern ambience. The work is therefore no 'concerto' in the virtuosic sense, although I regard Auden's poem as one of the most shattering examples of virtuosity in the history of English poetry.[14]

Bernstein also rejected the notion of a piece that relied for its meaning on imitative orchestration and dynamics, and yet he noted that

> when each section was finished I discovered, upon re-reading,
> detail after detail of programmatic relation to the poem—details
> that had 'written themselves'. Since I trust the unconscious
> implicity (sic), finding it a sure source of wisdom and the dictator
> of the condign in artistic matters, I am content to leave these
> details in the score. If the charge of 'theatricality' in a symphonic
> work is a valid one, I am willing to plead guilty.[15]

Bernstein divided the symphony into two parts, each with three sections: Part I consists of the Prologue, the Seven Ages, and the Seven Stages; Part II contains the Dirge, the Masque, and the Epilogue. All six sections include substantial piano solos except for the last movement (which, as I will explain, was much revised in 1965). Appropriately, both the Seven Ages and the Seven Stages movements take the form of variations on a theme. The instrumentation of the symphony includes woodwinds, brass, strings, percussion, harp, and pianino/celesta.

The Prologue begins with the twenty-two bars Bernstein composed in 1944 for Koussevitzky's birthday, now shaped as a duet for two clarinets. The contrasting voices evoke the solitary atmosphere of the bar on Third Avenue, "an unprejudiced space in which nothing particular ever happens," (p. 3) where the four protagonists sit in isolated self-reflection. In the poem, Quant wonders about the sadly resonant correspondences between music, emotion, and movement in the mirror-world behind the bar: "My deuce, my double, my dear image, / Is it lively there, that land of glass / Where song is a grimace, sound logic / A suite of gestures?" (p. 7). Auden's own interest in opera—he wrote several libretti, for instance—informs these first lines, and so does his opinion that the jukebox was "an instrument of torture invented in Hell."[16] Intrapsychically, Bernstein's two contrasting voices may be heard as consciousness and the unconscious, as a divided self.

In the second part of the Prologue, Bernstein presents a musical opposition that parallels Auden's four protagonists as they begin to interact. In his prefatory note, Bernstein describes the descending scale played by the flutes as acting "as a bridge into the realm of the unconscious, where most of the poem takes place." At the same time, in contrast, four quiet ascending chords convey the protagonists' first optimistic exchanges and their relief in having broken through their individual isolation with congenial talk.[17] The music moves down into the collective unconscious, and at the same time it alludes to the possibility of an ultimately purgatorial and ascendant outcome, appropriate for the setting of the action on the Night of All Souls.

In Auden's Seven Ages, Malin, as the thinking function, introduces each of seven phases of a human life, and then the other three functions play off his initial statements. Bernstein works differently.

> Each variation seizes upon some feature of the preceding one and develops it, introducing, in the course of the development, some counter-feature upon which the next variation seizes. It is a kind of musical fission, which corresponds to the reasonableness and didactic quality of the four-fold discussion.[18]

The seven variations progress, each theme linked to and building on its predecessor, all in patterns of ascent and descent. The conversation ends with an even more deeply descending scale, but then, inevitably, it reaches a C-major chord, which is Bernstein's musical translation of both Shakespeare's "sans everything" and Auden's "total extinction."[19] A narrative of the individual life, rendered in poetry or music, necessarily concludes with a statement of finality.

In the next movement, the Seven Stages, the variations correspond to the protagonists' responses to the seven psychic landscapes. Bernstein explains, "The characters go on an inner symbolic journey according to a geographical plan leading back to a point of comfort and security"—Quant's longing for "hope and health." "The four try every means, going singly and in pairs, exchanging partners, and always missing the objective. ... This set of variations begins to show activity and drive and leads to a hectic, though indecisive, close."[20] The seven variations accelerate, from the trudging march of a passacaglia to a waltz, then headlong from half notes to agitated quarter notes to racing eighth notes, culminating in the four final minor triad chords, then to hollow, expressionless octaves on C. The musical narrative expels the protagonists out of the potentially sacred liminality of the collective unconscious and back into the sadly profane setting of the bar where nothing of any significance can happen.

Bernstein first orchestrated and performed the fourth movement as an independent piece in a fund-raising concert in Tel Aviv on November 28, 1948. He then incorporated it into *The Age of Anxiety* as the Dirge. Bernstein writes, "This section employs, in a harmonic way, a twelve-tone row out of which the main theme evolves. There is a contrasting middle section of almost Brahmsian romanticism in which can be felt the self-indulgent aspect of this strangely pompous lamentation."[21] At this point in Auden's poem, the four voices form one voice; the protagonists who could not connect in their dream-quests can now experience a kind of unison in lamentation, in their shared sense of the loss of "health and hope." In Bernstein's symphony, the lamentation frames and thereby counters, even discounts, the evocation of a romantic semi-divine hero, some colossal father-figure who would "appear and impose peace on the pullulating / Primordial mess" (p. 104). Bernstein emphasizes the contrast between self-indulgence and pomposity; he trusts neither emotion, but he is interested in the void evoked between them. The Dirge culminates in the twelve notes sustained as a chord, played fortissimo. Here is the darkest point of Auden's poem and Bernstein's symphony, the stripped and unadulterated expression of individual and collective anxiety, of living as a solitary individual consciousness in a time of collective psychosis, in a world at war. Bernstein's music underlines the emotional and structural lowest point of the piece, rendering it more explicit than Auden's words.

In the Masque, the four agitated protagonists attempt to escape, in manic defense, from the existential anxiety they have been lamenting together in the taxi. Bernstein writes, "This is a scherzo ... in which a kind of fantastic piano-jazz is employed, by turns nervous, sentimental, self-satisfied, vociferous." The bluesy melody in F major is based on a song, "Ain't Got No Tears Left," cut from Bernstein's 1944 musical, *On the Town*; this title, unbeknownst to the listener, is perfectly appropriate musically and has an ironic sense for those who recognize it. Bernstein directs that it should be played "extremely fast" so that it feels driven.[22] He emphasizes the rising insistence behind the repetition of the tune, even as it's performed in differing moods, from "with warmth" to "with impetus" and then "with gusto." Finally, as the manic tune exhausts itself and recedes into the background, the solo piano, corresponding to Rosetta's soliloquy, is suddenly freed from the compulsive repetition of archetypal possession and is forced to face the solitude and confess "what is left beneath the emptiness."[23] The tremendous energy dissipates into nothing, and in a moment of theatre, the piano soloist sits, hands in lap, while a pianino in the orchestra thinly mimics the jazzy bravura of a few moments before. Bernstein described this as "a kind of separation of the self from the guilt of escapist living."[24] And yet, as Jungian analyst and dancer Stacy Wirth observes, this echoing of the jazz motif from the self back to the piano-protagonist is also potentially positive; it distills the merely manic element in the Masque into music that reflects back a positive life force, in a syncopated rhythm that Nazi Germany would have derogated as "degenerate."

The Epilogue states musically that whatever is left is "something pure," a faith that stands against the collective loneliness and anxiety. In his 1949 prefatory note, Bernstein writes, "At the very end, [the piano-protagonist] seizes upon it with one eager chord of confirmation, although he has not himself participated in the anxiety-experience leading to this fulfillment. The way is open; but, at the conclusion, is still stretching long before him."[25] Bernstein appears to privilege, as the climax of the symphony, Rosetta's epiphany through the feeling function, the realization of both her aloneness and God's covenant with her people. She can no longer hide from Him. The journey mapped in the stages of the poem has brought her (and only her) to this place and this realization. Ironically, God's omnipresence is both the cause of her anxiety and its resolution. In Bernstein's composition, only the feeling function can counter-address the anxiety produced by war, and this moment comes at the end of the Masque. By contrast, in the Epilogue, the four have again separated, and Bernstein seems to ask if Malin (as thinking function) has participated sufficiently in this experience of anxiety to grasp it as a core experience of psyche and bear witness to its countering fulfillment. The symphony ends with "a sudden statement of the newly-recognized faith," but for Bernstein this faith can only be prefigured or foreshadowed as a musical promise corresponding to Auden's image of Malin on the train emerging from the dark. The symphony ends with an oxymoron, a triumphant potentiality. The last phrases build slowly from pianissimo to triple forte, but they are also marked "with serenity." The pianist does not participate in the Epilogue's progressive statement of "something pure" but only shares in one last eager chord of confirmation.

The world premiere of the symphony took place in Boston on April 8, 1949, with the Boston Symphony Orchestra conducted by Koussevitzky and Bernstein playing the solo piano part. It was received well, but when it was performed in New York on February 23, 1950, with Lukas Foss at the piano and Bernstein conducting, it was dismissed as "wholly exterior in style, ingeniously conducted, effectively orchestrated, and a triumph of superficiality." Over time, pianists and critics expressed frustration particularly with the ending.

Pianists felt dissatisfied with their exclusion from the Finale. Critics found the triumphant conclusion clichéd and over-stated, in contrast to Auden's rhetorical restraint at the end of the poem.

Bernstein's friend and mentor Aaron Copland offered lukewarm praise: "At its worst Bernstein's music is conductor's music— eclectic in style and facile in inspiration. But at its best it is music of vibrant rhythmic invention, of irresistible élan, often carrying with it a terrific dramatic punch."[26] Musicologist Allen Shawn's comment was more insightful and empathetic: "To be sure, the work's connection to Auden was, if anything, even deeper than the composer let on, but this remarkable work might have been more likely to have been evaluated on its own merits had he titled it a piano concerto."[27] To what extent, then, did Bernstein's choice to call the piece a "symphony" distort the audience's expectations, so that (to borrow an image by Margaret Atwood on the pitfalls of criticism) critics encountering a musical giraffe assessed it according to the attributes (or lack thereof) of an elephant?[28]

In 1965, Bernstein revised the Epilogue so that it included the pianist more extensively, allowing the piano a cadenza before the coda. He wrote, "In the years since 1949, I have reevaluated my attempt to mirror Auden's literary images in so literal a way … I am now satisfied that the work is in its final form."[29] Shawn argues that Bernstein's revised piano ending takes up again the theme from the Prologue and transforms the descending scale motif into an ascending one, which is entirely suitable for a purgatorial narrative that begins on All Souls' Night and ends at dawn.[30] In her analysis of the symphony, Sarah Wallin Huff tracks how the piano's cadenza restates the serenity prefigured in previous sections and thus explicitly ties the work together as a whole.[31] It can also be argued that the strong conclusion of the Epilogue simply reflects a post-war optimism present in the younger composer that was absent in the older poet who had expurgated any inflated rhetoric from his *Collected Poems* and who had witnessed first-hand the devastation of Europe.

From the critical psychological perspective provided by Jung's typology, one could also argue that Auden, as an Introverted Thinking type, makes a space for Rosetta's (and his own inferior) feeling insight, but that he hands the Epilogue back to Malin's (and his own superior) thinking function. In contrast, Bernstein, as an Extraverted Feeling type, brings even more to the forefront Rosetta's Feeling insight as something new that transcends the collective anxiety expressed at the end of the Dirge and the compensatory defensive mania of the Masque.

What moral imperative will move collective consciousness forward out of the anxiety of wartime, out of the symphony's low point? Bernstein's answer insightfully emphasizes, even more than Auden's, the repressed feminine and its associations in Western cultures with an undifferentiated feeling function. This function expressed itself at the end of the symphony in a raw, even bombastic, manner that was aesthetically disconcerting but psychologically appropriate. It is the musical equivalent of Auden's image of the train—both say prophetically that this is the direction in which things could now move if any progress out of a darkly divided collective consciousness can be hoped for. (Alas, after 1947 the political direction headed towards more splitting, which resulted, as we know, in the Cold War.)

Shawn argues that Bernstein's own typology combined introversion and extroversion in equal measure, but that his public self was so dominant that it often appeared to be the whole man. Shawn says,

> In a sense he needed an audience for his introspective side and, unlike the classic introvert who gets energy from solitude, needed to store that audience within him when he retreated to his inner world to compose or study music. When he reemerged into the public sphere, he had a burning need to discuss the joys of complex art and poetry, to share his internal states and mystical longings, to make the internal external. Although interaction with collaborators was essential to him when he was writing his theater music, he seemed to need to enter a special, private state of mind to produce other works [such as *The Age of Anxiety*]. On many occasions he described ideas coming to him while lying down in contemplation, or sitting at the piano for hours on end in a kind of trance, from which he would awaken to find pages and pages of notes before him. These visionary trance states resembled those he entered while conducting, and from which he would have to return at the end of a performance.[32]

This character assessment suggests that Bernstein's conclusion to his *Age of Anxiety* symphony was deeply felt, collectively insightful, but critically misunderstood at the time.

These historical and psychological arguments address the composition in a biographical context. The aesthetic question remains: what to make of Bernstein's symphony now? I will have more to say about this in Chapter 4. In 2010, the critic Glyn Maxwell, writing in *The Guardian*, argued that Bernstein's *Age of Anxiety* was better than Auden's poem:

> Throughout the piece instruments explode into life, peter out suddenly or are drowned out by others, yet the same fragile theme struggles on. This gives the symphony the concision and the cohesion wanting in the poem. It is short (for a symphony) and electrifying. Its voices hear each other. And if the grand closing chords seem more resolved than anything at the end of the poem—notwithstanding Malin's Christian optimism as his train crosses the Manhattan bridge at sunrise—perhaps, at that point where genius in language and music meet, only the latter can seem to mend what's broken.[33]

JEROME ROBBINS, *AGE OF ANXIETY*: A BALLET, 1950

The Second Symphony became the foundation of dance works interpreting both Bernstein's music and Auden's poem. On February 26, 1950, the New York City Ballet premiered the earliest of these, choreographed by Jerome Robbins. Robbins toured this ballet for seven years, but then he banned all future remountings after a dispute with Bernstein. Consequently, it was excluded from the New York City Ballet's repertoire, and dance historians now classify *Age of Anxiety* as one of Robbins's "lost" ballets.[34] Even so, details of the choreography can be reconstructed from photographs, reviews, and interviews.

Robbins had previously collaborated with Bernstein on two ballets for Ballet Theater, *Fancy Free* (1944) and *Facsimile* (1946). He described *Age of Anxiety* as "a ritual in which four people exercise their illusions in their search for security. It is an attempt to see what life is about."[35] In the Prologue, in a public place in a large modern city, four people meet by chance. Their actions initially appear provisional and hesitant, but they find possibilities for stronger gestures in their discovery of each other, as if they become released in a physical sense by the hope of possible relationships. The journeys they take together function as metaphors (as figures, in dance terms) for their long exploratory exchanges in their attempts to understand themselves and their age, and the dance conveys these exchanges as movement. Dance historian Deborah Jowitt examined Robbins's copy of Auden's poem and notes how he picked out verbs that referred to emotional states that in turn could be translated into movement, and images that suggested spatial configurations.[36]

Figure 3: *Age of Anxiety,* **Jerome Robbins, Tanaquil Le Clercq, Roy Tobias, and Todd Bolender, choreography by Jerome Robbins, 1950, New York City Ballet, photograph by George Platt Lynes, courtesy of the Estate of George Platt Lynes and the New York Public Library.**

In Robbins's choreography, the Seven Ages section builds on Bernstein's seven variations in the first part of the symphony: infancy, adolescence, love, ambition, material success, disillusionment, and death. In the Seven Stages, Robbins introduces four additional figures, dressed like the four protagonists.[37] These doubles imitate the movements of the four characters, while lines of other masked figures parade by. In solos and pas-de-deux, the protagonists seek a sense of security or balance but find none. They emerge from the labyrinthine setting, first rejecting and pushing away their doubles, then connecting with the other three traveler-protagonists, with whom they now share the sense of having come through a common harrowing dream. In the Dirge, the Father figure appears like a mechanical giant on stilts, to whom they all turn in homage. This dark Nobodaddy props itself up by leaning on others, as the woman-protagonist dances before him, fascinated, much as Rosetta in the poem speaks of her father-daughter complex as both positive and problematic. In the dance, when the woman and the men kneel and reach out toward the dark figure, it topples over. The Masque marks their manic response to the loss of hope in this paternalistic leader. In the end, Robbins creates an Epilogue in which all four protagonists stand together as at the beginning of the ballet. They turn and move toward the four corners of the stage from which they first entered. And then, just before exiting, they turn back and bow tentatively to each other, as if to acknowledge something that they have given—and have been given—in the encounter with the others, in this anxious age.[3]

Figure 4: *Age of Anxiety*, **Jerome Robbins, Tanaquil Le Clercq, Roy Tobias, and Todd Bolender, Melissa Hayden, Herbert Bliss, Shaun O'Brien, Dick Beard, choreography by Jerome Robbins, 1950, New York City Ballet, photograph by George Platt Lynes, courtesy of the Estate of George Platt Lynes and the New York Public Library.**

The *New York Times* critic John Martin attended the premiere in February 1950 and praised the production:

> In the [Auden] poem there is a short peroration in which the
> poet seems to imply a return to mystical religion as the answer;

in Mr. Bernstein's music comes the dawn as a kind of glorious Technicolor, and Mr. Robbins's four figures simply bow to each other with a new peace, which has come from nowhere discernible and separate. It is a work that must be seen more than once before the fullness of its design becomes clear, for it is neither glib nor superficial. The 'seven ages' section seemed last night undefined and difficult to follow. From there on, however, there was a magnificent command of choreographic material and long-range design. The dream journey section is superbly done, the dirge for the superman concept is in excellent contrast, and the masque is a brilliant statement of a forced gaiety to blind one's self to one's own basic cynicism and fear. The four leading figures are in a sense shadowy in that they are not minutely characterized, but each has his sharp and distinctive color, and between them there evolves an intangible and potent dramatic line through the unrelated episodes.[39]

In *The New York Herald Tribune*, critic Walter Terry concurred:

It is an enormously compelling work of art. I cannot offer a synopsis, for it is not a story; it is an experience. The four who guide its course are the frightened souls of an anguished era and we share in their experiences, both real and imagined, as they find solace in passing proximity, as they recall and reject various ages of a lifetime, as they travel into dreams which melt in nightmares or nothingness, as they cry for a father-brother-dictator image to protect them, as they throw themselves into joyless revel, and as they finally find faith, or perhaps it is merely the promise of a faith to come, in their own frail beings. It is not, then, a story. It is an emotional experience communicated through dance, through Mr. Robbins's perceptive and eloquent dance.[40]

Charles Boultenhouse argues that in this work (and in the subsequent "Ballade," 1952) Robbins took up Ezra Pound's idea that music could serve as a criticism of poetry.[41] Extending this to consider choreography as a criticism of music, he said, "Jerome Robbins' choreography is both a superb critical exegesis of [Bernstein's] music and [Auden's] original poem,"[42] particularly in those moments when he augments or contradicts his poetic and musical sources. So, for example, in the dream journey, when Robbins introduces the doubles who mimic the protagonists, coloring their movements as narcissistic couplings even as they dance with others, the protagonists gain awareness and push this unreflective, vain mirroring aside, in search for a more direct connection. Most important, Robbins chooses to end with neither Auden's Malin as

Introverted Thinking function alone, nor with Bernstein's Rosetta as Extraverted Feeling function's statement of faith. Instead, Robbins provides an understated counterpoint between the four protagonists before they part. Boultenhouse interprets this intrapsychic ending as a critical challenge to the music and the poem.

Lincoln Kirstein reported that Auden disliked both Bernstein's Symphony and Jerome Robbins's ballet.[43] The New York City Ballet production traveled to London in the summer of 1950. It was remounted in November 1952 and revived briefly in January 1957, but, because of the falling-out between Robbins and Bernstein, it has never been seen again.[44]

JOHN NEUMEIER, *AGE OF ANXIETY*: HAMBURG BALLET, 1979

John Neumeier, the artistic director and chief choreographer of the Hamburg Ballet, is primarily a creator of large theatrical drama-based or narrative ballets who, in 1979, choreographed a ballet based on Auden's poem and Bernstein's symphony. In this work, Neumeier showed Auden's four characters as they come together in a bar to listen to the wartime news, and how they express their inner emotional states through the movements of the dance. In the souvenir program, Neumeier referred to Auden's reading of *Psychological Types* and acknowledged that the four main dancers were meant to depict Jung's four types of conscious functioning. The program also reproduces a black-and-white photomontage of New York and Hiroshima taken from the illustrations to Jung's book, *Man and His Symbols* (1969), as if to strengthen the references to Jung, to Auden's New York, and to the end of World War II.[45] Much of Neumeier's choreography explores the ways in which these four functions connect, resist, push against, lean on, and score off each other as a single entity. Neumeier takes this dynamic further; in his reworking of the poem, the four characters become five when the dream figure of God the Father joins the protagonists and the corps-de-ballet in the Dirge.

In 1990 Neumeier revisited and refashioned the choreography for Ballet West, for a program at the Kennedy Center, Washington, DC. *New York Times* reviewer Jennifer Dunning found the theme of the ballet best expressed in the set design by Zack Brown, when "the dark and glittering bar pulled away at one point to reveal a huge mirror that reflected the four characters on an icy, empty plain,"[46] as in a De

Chirico vista. Like Robbins, Neumeier highlighted Auden's interest in the theme of positive and negative mirroring by introducing four ghostly doubles who echo the protagonists back to themselves in empty gestures that parody the genuine complexity of their relationships.

Figure 5: John Neumeier's *Age of Anxiety*, Jane Wood as Rosetta, Robert Arbogast as Quant, Jeffrey Rogers as Malin, Kristopher Payne as Emble, 1990, photograph by Mikel Covey. Printed with permission of Boosey & Hawkes Collection/ArenaPAL.

LIAM SCARLETT, *THE AGE OF ANXIETY*: ROYAL BALLET, 2014

Liam Scarlett first read Auden's *Age of Anxiety* when he was fourteen years old. However daunting the text might have been for the adolescent, he intuited its importance, and much later, in 2014, as Royal Ballet Artist in Residence, he returned to Auden's poem through the music of Bernstein's symphony. He had choreographed a piece on World War I entitled "No Man's Land" (April, 2014) for the English National Ballet; here, in isolated juxtaposed settings, the men fight in the trenches and the women work in the munitions factories. Now Scarlett decided he wanted to address the cumulative effect of the two world wars on Eros, "builder of cities," and he remembered *The Age of Anxiety*.

Scarlett acknowledges the formidable intellectual challenges posed by Auden's poem. In an interview, he told me,

> I can't say that I understand every line of the Auden, but the images and sounds wash over you. Auden taught me not to worry about rendering the work comprehensible or explicit in terms of its meaning, but to trust sound and form and image as much as meaning, dramatic effect as much as idea.[47]

Scarlett formulates his poetic argument with movement and gesture, but he argues that movement needn't occur at the same time as Auden's literary or Bernstein's musical images; sometimes movement can anticipate them emotionally. He told another interviewer, "I like bringing in human emotion in dance, and I think it's amazing how the human body can express itself without words. Sometimes when words can't quite deliver what you want to say, body language takes over, even in normal, pedestrian everyday life."[48]

Scarlett however concurs with Auden's notion of poetic truth as dialectical and multi-voiced (as opposed to the single voice of a prose argument). He points to the four protagonists in the poem, reduced in Bernstein's symphony to a solo piano as the lone protagonist in dialectic with the orchestra, and in his choreography, Scarlett enjoyed reintroducing to the music the theatrical complexity of Auden's four protagonists. For the audience, this means the possibility of four different entry-points into the dramatic action and also the interbraiding of these perspectives as the dancers change partners and play off each other. Scarlett felt sure that different audience members would choose different protagonists with whom to identify, and that these identifications would shift and contradict one another as the narrative advances.

Scarlett researched the critical responses to the poem, and he understood the objections that the characters are not differentiated in tone or style, even if they are differentiated in the "stage directions" of the poem.

Scarlett's own interpretation, however, tends toward the interpersonal more than the intrapsychic. The sets by John Macfarlane are

Figure 6: Liam Scarlett, *The Age of Anxiety*, Laura Morera as Rosetta, Bennet Gartside as Quant, Tristan Dyer as Malin, Steven McRae as Emble, The Royal Ballet at the Royal Opera House, London, UK, photograph by Bill Cooper. Royal Ballet, ArenaPAL.

realistic: the bar scene nods to the hyper-realist painting "Nighthawks" (1942) by Edward Hopper, even though Hopper acknowledged the psychoanalytical features of his work.[49] So Macfarlane's set is very concretely a New York "dive," and yet it is also the appropriate setting for the protagonists' descent into the collective unconscious. Scarlett's choreography builds on this concreteness—the turning on and off of the jukebox, the sound of the bottles slammed down on the bar. At the same time, Scarlett introduces into this realism certain symbolic psychological elements, such as the sinister, diabolical movements of the bartender, as if he were the shadowy, undifferentiated god of the place. Is he Bacchus holding sway over the four anxious and intoxicated protagonists? Is he Hermes, god of exchanges (and god of thieves)? Or is he a dark Eros who will spark a possible connection among the four?

Scarlett builds the Seven Ages section of the ballet on the responses of the four protagonists to a soldier and his girlfriend who

Figure 7: Liam Scartlett, *The Age of Anxiety*, Bartender as prevailing god. Royal Ballet, ArenaPAL.

enter the bar for a drink. The protagonists are awakened, aroused, piqued, even provoked by the erotic moment they witness between the young couple, who dance to the jukebox music and then leave. Thrown back upon themselves, the four score off each other in Bernstein's increasingly frenzied variations: solos, pas-de-deux, trios, quartets. Eros as a fundamental human connection, as "builder of cities," feels embodied here in, the profane setting of the bar, but only as sexual permutation. Scarlett choreographs only one explicitly intrapsychic moment of connection: the dancers move from synchronized steps and gestures into a single unit of four bodies draped over each other on the floor, their breathing rising and falling in unison, reminiscent of Neumeier's interbraided configurations.

I asked Scarlett about the Romantic section of the Dirge, the musical interpretation of Auden's false myth of the Romantic hero who promises to save humankind, and Auden's own feelings of inauthenticity. Scarlett observed that Bernstein follows the linear sequence of Auden's structure but gives different weight to the sections so that, for instance, the Seven Ages and Seven Stages fly by, almost inconsequentially. The Dirge

> is the longest section; in Auden's poem it's a short taxi-ride to
> Rosetta's apartment. So I took the time to build the Dirge around
> the blocking of the four characters in the taxi, with Quant in the

front seat (someone has to sit in the front), and with Emble as the
sexual sailor seated in between Rosetta and Malin.[50]

Scarlett transposes what Bernstein referred to as "the two-pronged
Brahmsian Romantic lie and the self-indulgence" of the Lamentation
into a heavy, slow, ambiguous sexual tension. In the car-ride to the
Upper West Side, the possibility for eros, for authentic connection in
this profane and eristic wartime context, moves instead toward even
more aloneness. Here, at the end of the Dirge, Scarlett foreshadows
the choreographic outcome of the Masque, the emotional low point of
the piece. But first, as the Masque begins, the mania of the protagonists
builds with the dancers moving as if possessed. Increasingly exhausted,
they try to stop, but find themselves pulled back into the movement
by the others. The mania breaks only with a kiss between Rosetta and
Emble, which provokes Quant and then Malin to leave. In Auden's
poem, Rosetta, forced to forego making love when she discovers
Emble asleep, performs the compassionate maternal gesture of
covering him. Then she collapses into her solitary confession of
personal and collective anxiety. In Scarlett's ballet, this moment felt
undeveloped,[51] as if Rosetta's anxiety in the face of the war and the
Holocaust were mere sexual frustration.

Scarlett has constructed with Auden's foursome a kind of Sartrean
"hell is other people." Nobody connects. Even Quant, the most lonely of
them all, when back out on the street, offers to exchange addresses with
Malin and wants a kiss, but as soon as he departs, Malin throws away
the proffered business card. In his poem, the middle-aged Auden held
back at the end, closing with Malin's Thinking function underwritten
so that any affirmation might be found, not in the reasoned need for
religious faith but in the image of Malin's train emerging from darkness
into dawn. Bernstein, much younger, rendered more explicit the image
with the emotional correlative of a major seventh chord that the solo
piano repeats fortissimo back to the orchestra, as if to bravely counter
hateful Ares with the promise of resolution.

The Epilogue presented Scarlett with a significant choreographic
challenge. Scarlett looked for ways to balance Malin's anxious
soliloquy with Bernstein's affirmation and invented a solitary dance at
dawn for the jilted man. In the empty streets of New York, he expresses
the paradox of existential aliveness that moves from the dread of living
alone in a time of anxiety to gratitude for merely being alive. But by
following Auden's narrator's description and concluding with Malin

alone rather than with the four protagonists, the ballet loses some of its complexity. In this regard, perhaps Scarlett follows Auden and Bernstein too literally, in a too-linear fashion. He concludes his ballet, not with the intrapsychic complexity of the four, but with Malin's grandiose elation as he dances alone in the empty dawn streets of New York. Compared to Scarlett's, Robbins's choreographic critique of Auden and Bernstein's Epilogue, ending with all four characters present and the slightest suggestion of connection between them as they part, provides a more effective correlative in dance to its literary and musical sources.

Listening to the symphony and comparing notes on the three choreographies, I find that interpersonal interpretations highlight, as if by default, the importance of the intrapsychic: Malin is only one of four functions, so how can he take center stage by the Epilogue as the superior function in this psychological constellation? Working through these creative extrapolations back to Auden's poem, I appreciate even more that Jung's rational axis of Thinking and Feeling forms the spine of all these narratives, with Rosetta moving into place as the key player. Acknowledged or not, she voices the collective's way forward towards life.

NOTES

1. "I've just finished my book," Dec. 11, 1946, in Alan Ansen, *The Table Talk of W. H. Auden*, ed. Nicholas Jenkins (Princeton, NJ: Ontario Review Press, 1990), p. 8.

2. Jacques Barzun, in John Haffenden, ed., *Auden: The Critical Heritage* (London: Routledge, 1983), p. 366.

3. Delmore Schwartz, in Haffenden, *Auden*, p. 372. In the light of Auden's ethical struggle with editing his *Collected Poems* (see Chapter 1), it is interesting that in his review, Schwartz praises an early work that Auden disavowed as fascistic:

> It can be said that the most unique quality of modern literature is the eruption of the unconscious within areas of the conscious mind, which is not quite able to understand and control all that has forced its way up. It is significant that Auden now regards 'The Orators' as a failure while in writing 'The Age of Anxiety,' he strives to renew communication with the subject matter which made 'The Orators' one of his most exciting books. (Schwartz, p. 369)

Auden ethically distanced himself from *The Orators* (1931) because he judged he had written it as a kind of psychotherapeutic literary exorcism, discovering his own propensity for fascistic hero-worship and allowing himself to be possessed by it. In the Dirge section of *The Age of Anxiety*, Auden shuts the door on this once and for all: "Mourn for him now, / Our lost dad, / our colossal father" (p. 104).

4. *Times Literary Supplement*, Saturday, Oct. 23, 1948, vol. 596, no. 2438.

5. Leonard Bernstein, *The Leonard Bernstein Letters*, ed. Nigel Simeone (New Haven, CT: Yale University Press, 2014), pp. 230–31.

6. *Ibid.*, pp. 231–32.

7. "I'm amazed no one here knows what a 'gasometer' is. I wanted to use it for *The Age of Anxiety* and couldn't for that reason. I was heartbroken. I want the poem to be completely American in language." Ansen, *Table Talk*, p. 22.

8. Bernstein, *Leonard Bernstein Letters*, p. 228. Marketa Morris to Leonard Bernstein, Jul. 23, 1947:

> I don't think that our work will be finished in five months. But there is even some risk of your feeling worse after this period since many problems may have come into the open without finding a solution. Under the given circumstances I would want to start only if you are taking responsibility for such a possible outcome. Of course there is a chance that we may come to some essential clarification. No way to deny it. It's fifty fifty—and you have to know it. ... If you could give up Europe for the solution of your problems, you would have solved quite some of them and we had the most promising start. But would I make it a condition, which, I have to confess, was very tempting—I am sure it wouldn't work, since you would use it against me, that is, against our work.

9. *Ibid.*, pp. 249–50. Renée Noll to Leonard Bernstein, Jan. 20, 1949:

> Some short remarks on your dream: when you are unconscious ('taking a nap, sleeping'), you find that your rather undifferentiated feeling is playing tricks on you, bringing people into your psychology whom you do not want to have in there. Rather than finding out what these people really want from you, or why they were invited, you get angry at that side of yourself who played the trick on you. You get in touch with that side by hurting it, then you regret. You would know more if you would try to make her understand why you don't want these people anymore. Then, when you do get away from the unwanted collective, you get

into an even less desirable one, a very pedestrian collective (street). Being alone now, without anything but yourself, you are eager to make contact with some other side, contact in the usual average pedestrian way—sex—which is the substitute for human relationship. When you find that that is impossible you are caught in some very dull, past aspect of your own bourgeois side. That shows very nicely why you are so eagerly seeking homosexual contact in reality, it seems the way out or the escape from the fear of being caught in bourgeois patterns, and seems to symbolize the free and non-bourgeois life. They talk about your work in your dream; your fear always seems to be that being a conductor and being set in a profession is the same as being dully married and leading a middle-class life. I am sure it could be that way, but must not be that way, and will stop to look to you that way the moment you get some real color into your life; then you can give up the so-called 'colorful life' you are leading.

10. *Ibid.*, p. 273.

11. "Miss Nell" is his nickname for Renée Noll, just as "the Frau" was his nickname for Marketa Morris. *Ibid.*, p. 249.

12. Humphrey Burton, *Leonard Bernstein* (New York: Doubleday, 1994), p. 182.

13. Stephen Spender, "Afterword: Looking Back," in *World Within World* (New York: Modern Library, 1951/2001), p. 368. See also Burton Bernstein, "Family Matters II—The Kids," *The New Yorker*, Mar. 29, 1982, pp. 58–121.

14. Leonard Bernstein, prefatory note, *The Age of Anxiety* (Symphony No. 2): For Piano and Orchestra, After W. H. Auden (1949), Jalni Publications/Boosey & Hawkes, p. i.

15. *Ibid.*

16. Ansen, *Table Talk.*

17. Bernstein, prefatory note, *Age of Anxiety*, p. i.

18. *Ibid.*

19. For a detailed explication of Variations I–VII and VIII–XIV, I recommend Sarah Wallin Huff, "Leonard Bernstein's *The Age of Anxiety*, Symphony No. 2 (after W. H. Auden): History and Analysis" (2007). Accessed Jun. 9, 2015, at http://sarahwallinhuff.com/wp-content/uploads/2011/09/age-of-anxiety-final-paper.pdf.

20. Bernstein, prefatory note, *Age of Anxiety*, p. ii.

21. *Ibid.*

22. Allen Shawn, *Leonard Bernstein: An American Musician* (New Haven, CT: Yale University Press, 2014), p. 97.

23. Bernstein, prefatory note, *Age of Anxiety*, p. ii.

24. Program note, Apr. 8, 1949, quoted in Burton, *Leonard Bernstein*, p. 191.

25. Bernstein, prefatory note, *Age of Anxiety*, p. ii.

26. Aaron Copland, quoted in Shawn, *Leonard Bernstein*, p. 101.

27. Shawn, *Leonard Bernstein*, p. 100.

28. Nick Mount, "Interview: Elephants Are Not Giraffes: A Conversation with Margaret Atwood, More or Less about Northrop Frye," *University of Toronto Quarterly* 81 (1, 2012): 60–70.

29. Bernstein, prefatory note, *Age of Anxiety*, p. ii.

30. Shawn, *Leonard Bernstein*, p. 98.

31. Huff, "Leonard Bernstein's *The Age of Anxiety*," p. 24.

32. Shawn, *Leonard Bernstein*, pp. 196–97.

33. Glyn Maxwell, "W. H. Auden's 'The Age of Anxiety,'" *The Guardian*, Apr. 10, 2010, p. 4.

34. George Balanchine and Francis Mason, "Four Lost Robbins Ballets," *Ballet Review*, vol. 26, no. 3, Fall 1998, pp. 33–8.

35. *Ibid.*, p. 34.

36. Deborah Jowitt, *Jerome Robbins: His Life, His Theater, His Dance* (New York: Simon & Schuster), p. 164; see especially Jowitt interview with Bolander, Apr. 7, 2000, p. 165. Tom Bolander said,

> And then we reached out and touched each other this way [formally and reticently, yet inquisitively]. And then we did a grand plié, all four of us, with knees straight forward. And then we rose up and we dropped our arms and then we would look—I would look at you and you would look away from me. And [that pattern passed] right through the line and then back again until finally it ended back at this person and then we would look at each other across [the circle], like that. Then we started to back away from each other and then one person would start off in one direction and another and another and another. And then suddenly a sweep of dancers would come through and they would pick up one of the people.

In another interview, Bolander said: "[Jerry] seemed to focus on the very word anxiety in his movement—jagged, almost unrelated things, like tics sometimes, throughout the body." Bolander, in Reynolds, *Repertory in Review: 40 Years of the New York City Ballet*, p. 100, quoted in Jowitt, *Jerome Robbins*, p. 166.

37. Two of these masks, designed by Irene Sharaff, are preserved in the Jerome Robbins collection, New York Public Library, Performing Arts Division, Call Number *MGZGX.

38. A comment by critic Doris Hering in her review for *Dance Magazine* makes even more concrete a few of Robbins's choices. For example, in the dream journey designated as the Seven Stages, she describes the mirroring auxiliaries as dressed exactly like the principal characters so that they can observe and reflect upon themselves as they move: "The eight of them were tossed through a weird world of faceless beings. Yet the whole episode never sank into the sickly emptiness of most phantasmagoric representations." And in the Dirge, the four confront a shadowy gigantesque creature on stilt shoes to which they wish to submit themselves but which topples and disintegrates before their eyes. See also *Life Magazine*, p. 90, photograph by Philippe Halsman, "Tops in the Dance: New York's brilliant ballet becomes an ambassador of U.S. culture," in Jerome Robbins, "The Age of Anxiety," Clippings, *MGZR, New York Public Library, Performing Arts Division.

39. John Martin, *New York Times*, Feb. 28, 1950.

40. Walter Terry, *New York Herald Tribune*, Feb. 27, 1950. Years later, Walter Terry revisited the ballet and wrote that it "retains its formal strength, its quality of flowing inventiveness and its heart-touching emotional composition, virtues immediately apparent at its premiere several years ago." Jan. 28, 1957, Robbins, *Age of Anxiety*, *MGZR.

41. "The author's conviction of this day of New Year is that music begins to atrophy when it departs too far from the dance; that poetry begins to atrophy when it gets too far from music; but this must not be taken as implying that all good music is dance music or poetry lyric." Ezra Pound, *The ABC of Reading* (New York: New Directions, 1934/2010), p. 14.

42. Charles Boultenhouse, "The 'Poetics' of Jerome Robbins," *Ballet Review* 23 (2, 1995): 59–65; see esp. p. 62.

43. Lincoln Kirstein, *Thirty Years: Lincoln Kirstein's The New York City Ballet*, p. 76, in Jowitt, *Jerome Robbins*, p. 166.

44. A stage version of *The Age of Anxiety* was presented in New York by the Living Theater Studio in 1954. At Princeton, Theatre Intime, an undergraduate group, also staged an abridged version of the poem in 1960, with narrations played through a television on stage, and Auden agreed to serve as one of the narrators.

45. John Neumeier, souvenir program, *Songfest* and *The Age of Anxiety*, The Hamburg Ballet, Dec. 22, 1979 (Hamburg: Hamburgische Staatsoper, 1979), p. 70; and C. G. Jung, Marie Louise von Franz, John Freeman, *Man and His Symbols* (New York: Doubleday, 1969).

46. Jennifer Dunning, review/dance, "Neumeier Choreographs 'Age of Anxiety,'" *The New York Times*, Oct. 15, 1991. See also Dorothy Stowe, "Ballet West Offers a Neumeier Premiere," *Dance Magazine*, Sept. 1991, p. 15.

47. Liam Scarlett, Royal Ballet Artist in Residence, interview by Craig Stephenson, Koch Theater, New York City, Thursday, Jun. 25, 2015 at 11:00 am.

48. Liam Scarlett, quoted in Mary Ellen Hunt, "Liam Scarlett's smooth leap from corps to choreography," SFGate, Apr. 28, 2014. Accessed Jun. 27, 2015, at http://www.sfgate.com/performance/article/Liam-Scarlett-s-smooth-leap-from-corps-to-5431318.php.

49. Although he was a realist painter, Edward Hopper was interested in psychoanalysis and the power of the subconscious mind: "So much of every art is an expression of the subconscious that it seems to me most of all the important qualities are put there unconsciously, and little of importance by the conscious intellect." Sheena Wagstaff, ed., *Edward Hopper* (London: Tate Publishing, 2004), p. 71.

50. Scarlett, interview by Stephenson, Thurs., Jun. 25, 2015 at 11:00 am.

51. The Royal Ballet, Koch Theater, Lincoln Center, New York City, Saturday, Jun. 27, 2015 at 8:00 pm.

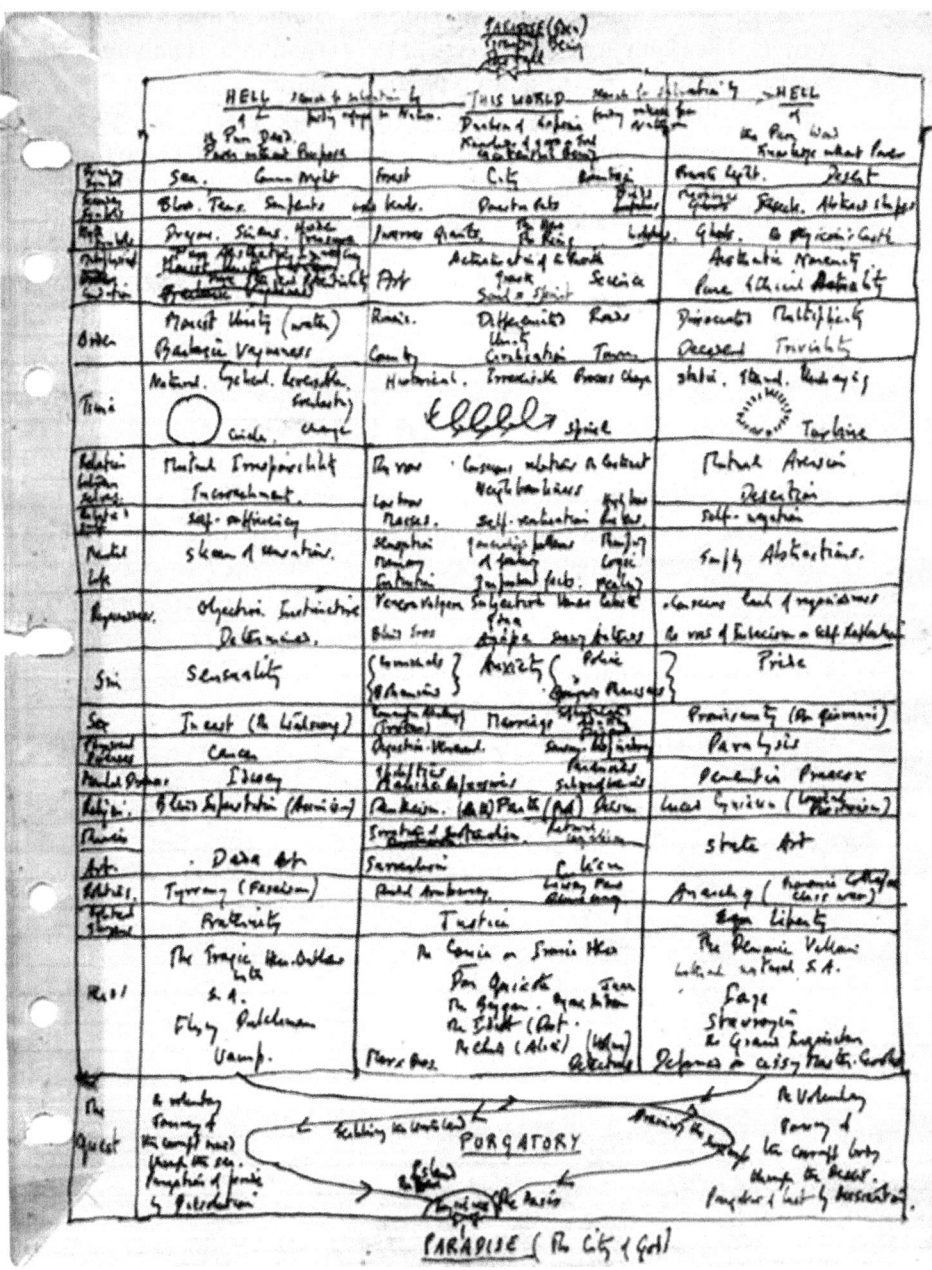

Figure 1: W. H. Auden, Chart for Swarthmore College lecture, 1943.

|||||||||||||||||||||||||||||||||||||||||||||||||||||||||||||||||||||||||||||||||||||||||||||||||||||||||||||||||||||||||||||||||||||||||

CHAPTER FOUR

CONCLUSIONS

A s a reader I've come rather late in life to Auden. It has been
wonderful to discover one of the great poets of the twentieth
century and, for me as a Jungian, to witness him make
intelligent and discriminating use of Jung's critical psychology of
type. Jung critiqued Western societies by noting the extent to which
they culturally over-identified with a single psychological function,
relegated the other functions to the shadows, and then experienced
them as inferior and negative. Jung compensated for this kind of
cultural one-sidedness by emphasizing opposites; in introverted
sensation-bound Switzerland, for instance, he promoted extraverted
intuition—irrational, image-based and timeless in its orientation—
and the importance of the symbolic life for psychological health.
Auden attuned himself to Jung's emphasis on metaphor and the
imagination as intuitive ways of knowing and on Jung's model
of the personality as naturally inclined towards integration and
wholeness (in the same way that the body inclines naturally towards
healing). At the same time, Auden warned against the Romantic
imaginative inclination that led to elitist and fascistic outcomes,
such as the Nazi dredging up of Viking mythology to vindicate its
gangster ethics. Like Jung, the middle-aged Auden qualified his
interests in types and teleology.[1]

Auden conducted literary experiments with Jung's psychological
types during various stages of his writing life. In *The Age of Anxiety*,
for example, he set (as we saw) a particular constellation of four in

motion and tracked the poetic outcome, exploring how far Jung's four functions could go when traveling in the borrowed vehicle of a baroque eclogue. In this regard, the American poet James Merrill said he learned from Auden how to work as a formalist, choosing a set of variables and then relinquishing control of the emergent dialectic to reach a poetic truth: "I by and large put my faith in forms. The attention they require at once frees and channels the unconscious, as Auden kept reminding us. Even if your poem turns out badly, you've learned something about proportion and concision and selflessness."[2] For Auden, poetic truth is necessarily multi-voiced and interrelated and inclusive, as is psychological truth for Jung.

In her essay, "Auden as Philosopher: How Poets Think," Jan Zwicky emphasizes Auden's fervent belief in the humanities as evidence of our humanizing impulse, and in the love of language for its own sake, as well as in the negotiation between private vision and public understanding in the search for difficult truths:

> Auden offers an anthropological argument: in cultures that acknowledge a social distinction between the sacred and the profane, poets have a public role. In cultures that don't make this distinction, the poet has no public role, and poetry is intimate. In cultures that value the sacred, the poet is held in high regard; in cultures that disparage the sacred, the poet too is disparaged and marginalized.[3]

Zwicky charts how Auden borrows Coleridge's distinction between Primary and Secondary Imagination to define an epistemology of the imagination. Primary imagination perceives sacred beings and sacred events in a receptive attitude of awe; secondary imagination perceives not the sacred but beauty, and it is actively articulate and social. Zwicky identifies this distinction within a Freudian taxonomy of primary and secondary psychological processes or concerns.[4] Auden's reading of Jung apparently finds no place in Zwicky's argument. And yet a Jungian taxonomy would differentiate precisely between visionary art as primal, public, and sacred, and psychological art as personal. Indeed, as Auden knew, poets give voice, in varying degrees and combinations, to collective cultural concerns and to the collective unconscious, as well as to personal experience and memory.[5] As Zwicky points out, the problem for Auden's poetry (and for Jung's psychology as well) is that in Western cultures thinkers disparage an epistemology of the imagination because it generates truths that are not evidence-based.

The intuition-based imagination aims not to prove but to praise. And a truth that is articulated publicly as numinous will be denigrated as either inflated and affected or idiosyncratic and personal.

Jung avoided Freud's generalizing view that all anxiety was sexually based, but he himself tended towards generalizing anxiety as symptomatic of an avoidance to become conscious of genuine suffering. In practicing psychotherapy, Jung tracked anxiety in order to identify possibilities that patients had evaded in their lives. Samuels, Shorter, and Plaut note,

> There is little doubt that Jung did not deal adequately with the various defensive processes employed by the ego to ward off anxiety. This may be partially attributed to his equating of 'ego' with 'consciousness.' This meant that the possibility that parts of the ego's structure are themselves unconscious is not entertained. It is these unconscious ego defenses which deal with anxiety.[6]

But Jung put forth the therapeutic notion of supporting the patient's ego so that it could come to bear the truth about itself, including its relatively inferior position within the psychic structure: "we forge an ego that does not break down when incomprehensible things happen; an ego that endures, that endures the truth, and that is capable of coping with the world and with fate."[7] Jung's interest in a religious attitude connected to this capacity of the ego to endure its relationship to the self as God-image. He writes,

> As Kierkegaard says, 'before God man is always wrong.' By fear, repentance, promises, submission, self-abasement, good deeds, and praise he propitiates the great power, which is not himself but *totaliter aliter*, the Wholly Other, altogether perfect and 'outside,' the only reality.[8]

As I mentioned, around the time of the composition of *The Age of Anxiety*, Auden criticized the anti-religious bias of orthodox Freudian psychoanalysis. He saw its increasingly rationalist agenda as discharging the individual out into the adult world, bereft not only of childish illusions and transferences but also of poetic truth, of a dialectic that includes the possibility of a numinous discourse. If an experience of healing in psychotherapy manifests itself with accompanying religious connotations of transcendence or transformation, and if the analyst rejects any discourse colored by such tones, then the powerful affective change may be repressed and will manifest itself negatively in the transference as mere power.

> Psychotherapy will not get much further until it recognizes that
> the true significance of a neurosis is *teleological*, that the so-called
> traumatic experience is not an accident, but the opportunity for
> which the child has been patiently waiting—had it not occurred,
> it would have found another, equally trivial—in order to find a
> necessity and direction for its existence, in order that its life may
> become a serious matter. Of course it would be better if it could
> do without it, but unconsciously it knows that it is not, by itself,
> strong enough to learn to stand alone: a neurosis is a guardian
> angel; to become ill is to take vows.[9]

We would be justified in assuming that this figure of speech—neurosis
as *angel*—belongs to Jung's vocabulary of complexes, among other
metaphorical terms such as *demons* and *possession*, but we would be
mistaken. The image is Auden's.[10]

An ongoing problem in the Jungian critical interpretation of
art and literature has been that Jungian interpreters traditionally
position the works of art within a Jungian frame and then make the
works serve that frame, as if art should exist to justify and legitimize
analytical psychology. Much Jungian criticism has consisted in
dutifully identifying shadows and animas, and in mapping narratives
to prove the prevalence of Jung's individuation process.[11] I've tried to
work differently here, taking up Auden as a writer who deliberately
employed Jungian concepts and showing how, unless we study Jung's
oeuvre seriously, we might not only misrepresent Jung's concepts but,
more importantly, misinterpret Auden's.

The Age of Anxiety depicts a subjective, intrapsychic process
rather than an objective, interpersonal one: in a dream, one doesn't
expect a personified figure to be multi-faceted or well rounded. Once
this is established, critical complaints about Auden's failure to write
differentiated characters fall away. As a result, the poem's formal
structure comes to the foreground and takes precedence over dramatic
representation, with the four functions moving through archetypal
landscapes and combining in patterns that spark a number of emotions:
hope, loss, anxiety, and even mania as defense against emotion.

In their extrapolations from Auden, composer Bernstein and
choreographers Robbins, Neumeier, and Scarlett render even more
explicit these structural progressions and the emotions evoked in the
poem. In Rosetta's soliloquy at the end of the Masque, for instance,
Feeling, undervalued and now unmasked, addresses itself directly to
the Godhead. In the symphony and the choreographies, even more

than in the poem, we witness a strong feminine response to Western patriarchy and to the collective catastrophe of the Second World War. Auden's experiment seems to formulate, like the lysis of a dream, that this is one way in which things could move forward from the annihilating effect of war on morality and human sensibility.

Alan Jacobs complains that Jung's types are merely heuristic descriptions of our human condition,[12] but he doesn't mention that Jung acknowledged this about his and all taxonomies. As editor of the most recent edition, Jacobs assesses *The Age of Anxiety* as important but at the same time describes it as an obscure psychological poem that no one can get through.[13] In his essay "From Myth to Parable," Edward Mendelson admits that he dislikes Auden's visionary rhetoric and its Jungian sources, and he expresses relief when Auden moves beyond his explicitly Jungian phase.[14] John Fuller, on the other hand, readily identifies the Jungian elements in Auden's work, not as an anomaly but simply as one of many through-lines that readers can track and weigh and interpret. And then there is Auden himself, who notoriously edited his work, changing words and phrases and deleting entire poems from his oeuvre, and yet who did not excise the Jungian "Four Faculties" from *For the Time Being*, even though he wrote "BOSH" in the margin of someone's copy; whether this applied to Jung's concept or to his own lines we can't tell. Nor did he reject *The Age of Anxiety*, even though he deleted from his *Collected Works* "September 1, 1939," his earlier piece of war-work, also set in a bar in New York City, because he deemed it "an outright lie."

As I mentioned in Chapter 1, when Auden was struggling with his studies at Oxford, he told his tutor Nevill Coghill that he was going to be, not simply a poet, but a great one. The English boarding school taught students humility and deference to "one's elders and betters," so it's not surprising that Auden's youthful determination to honor a poetic calling or vocation expressed itself (and was received by Coghill) as a presumptuous audacity. In his 1939 essay, "The Public v. the Late Mr. William Butler Yeats," Auden evaluates when poets merit the public designation of "great":

> To deserve such an epithet, a poet is commonly required to convince us of three things: firstly a gift of a very high order for memorable language, secondly a profound understanding of the age in which he lives, and thirdly a working knowledge of and sympathetic attitude towards the most progressive thought of his time.[15]

I hope, if nothing else, this investigation of Jungian inspiration in *The Age of Anxiety* makes evident the extent to which Auden met the standard of his own criteria for greatness. As war-work, *The Age of Anxiety* manifests a profound understanding of its time and an imaginative commitment to affirming humanity (without self-righteousness or bombast) in a compensatory act of poetic faith performed, against despair, in response to the devastation.[16] It also demonstrates, in line after line, "a gift of a very high order for memorable language."

What then would Auden himself have considered a failure? While finishing *The Age of Anxiety*, he spoke about this question in an address on Henry James at the Grolier Club:

> Those who attempt to become creative artists and fail may be divided into three classes: Firstly, those who have no talent; secondly, those who are seduced by their natural longing for what Freud so mistakenly believed to be the lure of all artistic creation, honor, power, and ... the goods of this world; and thirdly, and most tragically, those who are seduced by the devil's subtlest temptation, the desire to do good by their art.[17]

Clearly, Auden knew from experience the temptation of the third. His inclination to affirm could manifest in the pontificating of the "Court Poet of the Left" and in the concomitant risk of inauthenticity, employing inflated rhetoric in service of a good cause. In *The Age of Anxiety*, Auden succeeded in affirming faith without falling victim to either the light of worldly acclaim or the dark of doing good.

In June of 1945, around the same time that Auden was traveling in war-torn Germany before returning to New York to complete *The Age of Anxiety*, Jung was lecturing at the Psychological Club in Zürich about the French Romantic poet Gérard de Nerval. For Jung, Nerval was a poet who had failed in yet a different sense from those listed by Auden: as a personality who could not profit psychologically in his life from the extraordinary visionary insights in his art.[18] For Jung, Nerval's visionary memoir *Aurélia*, written at the request of his psychiatrist as an attempt to articulate his way out of psychosis and mental alienation, was a work of "extraordinary magnitude," but writing *Aurélia* didn't save Nerval from suicide. In his essay on the transcendent function, Jung describes two groups of clients. Some need to experience the autonomy of the unconscious without interpreting it; others need to experience the unconscious aesthetically, in creative self-expression, and also to appreciate its moral imperative with regard to how they live their lives.[19] Certainly Jung understood this in connection with his own experiments in *The Black Books* and *The Red Book*: how to write a literary work explicitly for a psychological rather than an aesthetic purpose, and how to transmute insight into action. Auden too came to understand that his life and his artistic work were inextricably linked, that failure in one realm meant failure in the other. He wrote that "the relation of Life to Work is dialectical, a change in the one presupposes and demands a change in the other."[20] At the same time, as I mentioned, Auden knew how to differentiate between the two (perhaps more carefully than either Nerval or Jung) and not fall into the mistake of treating his life as if it were a work of art to be edited and concluded. Life, unlike art, is greedy of experience.[21]

Using Jung's critical psychology of types, Auden addressed the meaning of anxiety in his time. Mapping anxiety on Jung's rational axis of Thinking and Feeling and the irrational axis of Intuition and Sensation, he narrated the effort required to arrive at stripped-down, differentiated psychological functions where consciousness can experience fear and faith in response to an uncertain future. In Auden's formulation, at the end of the long journey on All Souls' Night, Malin and Rosetta's monologues mark the point at which the narrative turns to looking up and ahead.[22]

Malin speaks as the superior function of Thinking, a function Jung often identified as close to patriarchal Western collective consciousness and to the concept of a Logos principle. Rosetta's speaking is more laborious, representing the undervalued function of Feeling in patriarchy. This can be formulated in Jungian terms as the oft-neglected voice of an Eros principle that brings together what Logos has separated analytically into parts, or as anima that offers to ego consciousness images of the archetype of life. The cumulative effect of the voices of Malin and Rosetta changes the direction and the tonal quality of Auden's poem; anxiety as a psychological defense against fear of meaninglessness—of being thrown into the fire like a weed—is rendered meaningful by the significance of the individual life. No deity manifests itself in a whirlwind to answer Rosetta and Malin, but the implicit presence of God as image alters the narrative from a long night-journey to the possibility of a dawning and a different kind of dialogue. Psychologically, through this work, Auden finds his typological spine, extending down from his superior function to his inferior function.[23] Politically, the work counters the fascistic forces both in the world and in Auden's shadow that promise security in exchange for the loss of democratic principles and the rights of the individual. Even more emphatically than Auden, Bernstein in his symphony privileges Rosetta's soliloquy with her articulation of the paradox of faith and her valuing of life rather than power.[24] Robbins, Neumeier, and Scarlett grapple creatively with the challenge of how best to enact this potential for change.

Rosetta's soliloquy is also a prophecy: "Odourless ages, an ordered world / Of planned pleasures and passport-control, / Sentry-go sedatives, soft drinks and / Managed money, a moral planet / Tamed by terror" (p. 17). It is we whom Rosetta questions: how are we to endure anxiety in our time and refuse to be "tamed by terror?"

Kierkegaard provided Auden with an ironic re-valuing of anxiety: "It is an adventure that every human being has to live through, learning to be anxious so as not to be ruined either by never having been in anxiety or by sinking into it. Whoever has learned to be anxious in the right way has learned the ultimate."[25] In Kierkegaard, Auden found an Introverted Thinking argument about how best to endure anxiety as a necessary condition of creative existence. Auden had already distanced himself from Freud's position in *The Problem of Anxiety* (1926), judging that the outcome of orthodox psychoanalytical treatment was insufficient for the individual ego that must learn to bear the truth about itself. During the war years, while he was composing *The Age of Anxiety*, Auden revisited Jung and Kierkegaard, as well as the theologians Reinhold Niebuhr and Paul Tillich.[26] After the Second World War, at least for a time, the Kierkegaardian denotations of the word *anxiety* remained viable, most famously in the philosophical and psychoanalytic argument of Rollo May's *The Meaning of Anxiety* (1950), steeped in the post-Freudian writings of Otto Rank, and in the work of Holocaust survivor Viktor Frankl's *Man's Search for Meaning* (1959).

But the signifier *anxiety* was already beginning to change considerably during that time. The five successive editions of the American Psychiatric Association's *Diagnostic and Statistical Manual of Mental Disorders* provide a map with which to track the changes in this discourse. In the first edition of the *DSM*, published in 1948, psychodynamic-based psychiatric theory identified combinations of anxiety and depression (and their concomitant somatizing possibilities) as caused by conflicts between consciousness and the unconscious; the term *psychoneurosis* covered both anxiety and depression as mechanisms of pathology. By 1968, in the second edition, *psycho* had been deleted, perhaps because etymologically it was implicit in the word *neurosis*, which denotes a non-organic abnormality of the nerves. By the third edition in 1980, the editors entirely deleted the word *neurosis* from the manual in an attempt to identify disorders by descriptors of behaviors rather than by causal notions of unconscious mechanisms. So, anxiety and depression now were given their places as fully differentiated psychiatric disorders even though they often manifest together (that is to say, in psychiatric terms, are *co-morbid*). Most recently, the fifth edition (2013) defines *generalized anxiety* as a disorder that manifests as a period of involuntary anticipatory worry accompanied by three or more persistent problems including restlessness, fatigue, problems of concentration, irritability, muscle tension, and sleep disturbance.[27]

The editors of the *DSM* have contributed to the positive differentiation of anxiety as a mental disorder, but they are also implicated in a serious distortion of the term. Their definitions of the anxiety disorders entered the third edition of the *DSM* concurrent with the introduction into the marketplace of anti-anxiety medications produced by pharmaceutical companies. More precisely, the diagnostic descriptions were predicated on the medications. By now, this kind of collusion between psychiatry and the pharmaceutical industries is explicit, indeed, assumed. Multinational companies benefit from psychiatry's claim that its nosology in the *DSM* is universal and complete, and they fund psychiatric research conducted in universities but suppress the publication of scientific results that do not support their projected outcomes. Anxiety in the United States is big business: forty million Americans are diagnosed with anxiety disorders every year. And pharmaceutical companies and insurance companies want to convince the rest of the world that, outside the United States, the condition is under-diagnosed and that its sufferers could, with the help of medication, obtain relief from their misery. Meanwhile, the biomedical definition of anxiety—hyperactivity in the amygdala with reduced activity in the frontal cortex—appears to support the cognitive/behavioral school of clinical psychology's operational definition of anxiety: a conditioned fear response that can be eliminated not with medication but with exposure therapy and Cognitive Behavior Therapy. Memoirs of anxiety and journaling workbooks by clinical psychologists fill the psychology sections of bookstores and book websites.[28]

My Age of Anxiety: Hope, Dread, and the Search for Peace of Mind is the title of a memoir by Scott Stossel (2013). It describes the author's personal experiences of anxiety, his years of suffering and his treatments, his research into the history of anxiety and theories about its transmission (whether genetic or through inadequate primary attachments by anxious parents), and his concern for his own children. He surveys the complex literature on anxiety and positions treatment strategies on a continuum ranging between two extremes: *cosmetic psychopharmacology* in which anxiety is recognized as a medical problem and a correctable chemical imbalance (which in the end is not borne out by Stossel's review of the research) and *pharmacological Calvinism*, a term coined by an angry psychiatrist to describe the elitism inherent in the philosophical and psychoanalytic notion of anxiety as meaningful, if only to a privileged few.[29]

Stossel tries to differentiate between the Generalized Anxiety Disorder 300.02 (F41.1) defined psychiatrically in the current *DSM-5*[30] and the kind of global anxiety described "psychologically" by Kierkegaard as fear in the face of possibility. To what extent are mental and somatic distresses, in such debilitating forms as agoraphobia or panic, valid responses to the intuition of too many possibilities?[31] The psycho-medicalized frame (constructed using anti-anxiety medication) and the psychotherapeutic frame (of professional alliance using regular sessions and repeated gestures) both work to give patients security, to reduce their symptoms of anxiety so that they can survive the day-to-day without feeling utterly disordered. But eventually, once patients feel sufficiently contained and buttressed, essential questions arise: how to choose between permanently dampening anxiety with medication and reprogramming with cognitive behavior techniques, or how to endure the anxiety, in Kierkegaard's existentialist sense, enough to replace it with awareness of the dizzying freedom to choose (which is its cause)? To what extent do treatments of anxiety reduce consciousness, and when is this a desirable end and not merely a means? In light of these concerns, Stossel might read Auden's *Age of Anxiety* with its Jungian model as a proposal for an optimal outcome: the differentiation and refining of conscious functions and the dawning of yet more consciousness.

Stossel comes to trust Dr. Barry E. Wolfe as his most effective therapeutic ally through the decades of his ailment. As the author of *Understanding and Treating Anxiety Disorders*,[32] Wolfe seems to have supported Stossel's decision to publish an anxiety memoir as a meaningful attempt to write his way out of his suffering. Wolfe's response—"You can write yourself to health"—echoes precisely Dr. Émile Blanche's response in 1854 to Nerval's decision to write a memoir about his psychotic episodes in order to contradict their alienating effects (or Jung's similar work with active imagination in the writing of his *Red Book*). In his book, Stossel's experiences are both personal and public; the introverted protagonist suffers terribly as he uneasily catapults himself into the demands of extraverted American society, fearing his body's vulnerability.[33] Stossel wrestles within bankrupt discourses of anxiety that produce only closed or sterile binary dialectics of public versus private. Decades of attacks by psychiatry, clinical psychology, and pharmaceutical companies on psychoanalytic and experiential practices have succeeded in diminishing patients' accessibility to the kind of transitional third spaces where discourse can engender what Auden would have called the "poetic truth" and lead to the possibility of change. In the light of *The Age of Anxiety*, it is fascinating to see, in Stossel's *My Age of Anxiety*, how Wolfe steers his patient over and over again in the direction of more and even more differentiated consciousness.[34]

As a solitary poet in exile, as an introverted English resident alien in New York, Auden imaginatively contradicted the tyranny of nationality with images of a new cosmology he devised himself. "Assuming that the artist, the writer today, decides rightly or wrongly, to continue pursuing his vocation, what are his obligations? To this question, Henry James offers, I believe, the correct answers. He must become international and he must stand alone."[35] Here, Auden describes quite consciously his own fate as a writer. He left Britain in order to avoid being swallowed by the British literary establishment. He took up American citizenship immediately after the war but regarded himself not as an American but as a citizen of New York City. And nationalism was anathema to him. Nicholas Jenkins emphasizes the forcefulness of Auden's critique of nationalism and of the passport as the modern indicator of identity.[36]

Already in the remarkable 1935 essay, "Psychology and Art Today," which recommends two books by Jung, Auden mapped a modernist cosmology in a chart as dense and provocative as that of his Dante. In 1943, for a class he was teaching at Swarthmore College, he expanded the chart and rendered it more complex.[37]

As far back as his 1928 Berlin sojourn, Auden had started devising such charts, some taken from Homer Lane's teachings, some from his conversations with John Layard. These charts showed the causes of crime, disease, and madness as lying (according to Auden) in the upsetting of the psychodynamic balance between the conscious and unconscious halves of the mind. Another chart in his 1930 notebook works out the relationship between somatic disease and psychological illness, and a glossary of Christian and psychological terms constructs analogies between the discourses of Christianity and psychology. In it, Heaven represents the unconscious, Earth the conscious mind, Hell is the repressed unconscious, the Father the ego-instincts, the Son the death-instincts, the Holy Ghost the libido, and the Archangels the four great ganglia of the body, a term borrowed from D. H. Lawrence.[38] His cosmology is an Introverted Thinking-Intuitive's guide to the universe.

The chart continued to grow in complexity. By 1943, in terms of his own type profile, Auden was struggling both to understand Chester Kallman's sensation-based rejection of fidelity in favor of masochistic anonymous sexual encounters and to discover how to honor the genuine eros in Rhoda Jaffé's offer of love. As a result, Auden eventually introduced Eros and Anteros, Eros' vengeful brother, into his revised cosmology, just as, in his life, he adopted an anterotic stance towards Chester Kallman, taking up the compensatory position of "the more loving one" in the erotic tug of war between lover and beloved.[39] And just below Eros and Anteros, at the center of Auden's cosmology is "Anxiety," with "Criminals" and "Bohemians" fleeing from it to the left into Sensuality, and with "Police" and "Bourgeois Pharisees" fleeing from it to the right into Pride. All this to say, in *The Age of Anxiety*, Auden provides readers with a complex symbolic cosmology as an antidote against eristic times, against divisive nationalisms, and against possession by dangerous archetypes (see Appendix).

In a 1944 *New York Times* review of a new edition of Grimm's tales, Auden makes his point of view even more explicit. He recommends the tales as an educational necessity for all adults:

> I think one must ... state as emphatically as the Nazis that Folk and
> Democracy are incompatible notions. To belong to a Folk means
> to have a group rather than an individual personality, whether the
> former be politically or occupationally determined. Democracy,
> it should be realized, is a very severe mistress. For Democracy
> demands unconditionally and all the time, of everyone that he or

PARADISE
(Eden)
Essential Being

The Fall

	HELL of the Pure Deed, Power without Purpose ← Search for Salvation by finding refuge in Nature →		THIS WORLD, Dualism of Experience, Knowledge of Good and Evil, Existential Being		← Search for Salvation by finding release from Nature → HELL of the Pure Word, Knowledge without Power	
Primary Symbol	Sea	Common Night	Forest	City	Mountain	Private Light Desert
Secondary Symbols	Blood Tears Serpents		Wild Beasts Domestic Pets		Birds	Machines Insects Abstract shapes
Myth Symbols	Dragons Sirens Hidden Treasure		Dwarves Giants The Hero The Ring		Witches	Ghosts The Magician's Castle
Metaphysical Condition	Pure Aesthetic Immediacy Pure Ethical Potentiality		Art Actualization of the Possible, Growth, Soul=Spirit		Science	Aesthetic Nonentity Pure Ethical Actuality
Order	Monist Unity (water) Barbaric Vagueness		Rivers Country Differentiated Unity Civilization		Roads Town	Dissociated Multiplicity Decadent Triviality
Time	Natural Cyclical Reversible Everlasting Circle change		Historical Irreversible Spiral	Process Change	Static	Eternal Unchanging Turbine
Relation between Selves	Mutual Irresponsibility Encroachment		The Vow Conscious relations Neighborliness The Contract			Mutual Aversion Desertion
Relation to Self	Self-sufficiency		Low brow Masses Self-Realization High brow Rulers			Self-negation
Mental Life	Stream of Sensations		Sensation Memory Intuition Generalized patterns of feeling, Important facts Thinking Logic Feeling			Empty Abstractions
Requiredness	Objective Instinctive Determined		Venere Vulgare, Blind Eros Subjective Grace, Agape Venere Celeste, Seeing Anteros			Conscious lack of requiredness, The void of Indecision or Self-Reflection
Sin	Sensuality		Criminals / Bohemians Anxiety Police / Bourgeois Pharisees			Pride
Sex	Incest (The Walsung)		Romantic Adultery (Tristan) Marriage Sophisticated Adultery (Figaro)			Promiscuity (Don Giovanni)
Physical Diseases	Cancer		Digestive-Venereal Sensory-Respiratory			Paralysis
Mental Diseases	Idiocy		Epileptics Manic-Depressives Paranoiacs Schizophrenics			Dementia Praecox
Religion	Blind Superstition (Animism)		Pantheism (Cath.) Faith (Prot.) Deism			Lucid Cynicism (Logical Positivism)
Theories			Irrational Emotionalism Rational Legalism			
Art	Dada Art		Surrealism Cubism			State Art
Politics	Tyranny (Fascism)		Feudal Aristocracy Laissez Faire Democracy			Anarchy (Economic Collapse Class War)
Political Slogans	Fraternity		Justice			Liberty
Hero	The Tragic Hero-Outlaw with S[ex] A[ppeal] Flying Dutchman Vamp		The Comic or Ironic Hero, Don Quixote, The Beggar, The Idiot (Dost.), The Child (Alice) Byron's Don Juan Marx Bros. Detectives (Holmes)			The Demonic Villain without natural S[ex] A[ppeal], Iago, Stavrogin, The Grand Inquisitor, Depraved or Cissy Master-Crooks
The Quest	The Voluntary Journey of the corrupt mind through the Sea. Purgation of pride by Dissolution		Fertilizing the Wasteland PURGATORY Draining the Swamp The Island Forgiveness The Oasis			The Voluntary Journey of the corrupt body through the Desert. Purgation of Lust by Dessication

PARADISE
(The City of God)

Figure 2: W. H. Auden, Chart for a seminar on romanticism at Swarthmore College, 1943. Transcription by Edward Mendelson.

> she become a conscious, responsible individual. To the People,
> Democracy is never at home; she is only 'in' to a voluntary
> association of persons. ... Whoever today, whether in arts or
> politics, idolizes the folk-like and popular and disparages the
> highbrow and difficult, is making, whether he means to or not,
> propaganda for the Police State. ... Half of our troubles, both
> individual neuroses and collective manias such as nationalism,
> seem to me to be caused largely by our poverty of symbols,
> so that not only do we fail to relate one experience to another
> but also we have to entrust our whole emotional life to the few
> symbols we do have.[40]

In this sense, what Auden mapped for his students at Swarthmore
College as a cosmology was in fact a protective antidote against the
dearth of meaningful symbols in their times. *The Age of Anxiety*, too,
is steeped in this restorative, symbol-laden cosmology.

Of course, planting this cosmology into collective consciousness
as a poetic truth was doubly urgent. What followed the Second World
War was neither compensatory receptiveness to an Eros principle
nor any privileging of the collective feminine, but instead a Cold
War that led to even more collective splitting, with the building of
nuclear arsenals and the Berlin Wall. Auden wisely underwrote his
conclusions. He contributed an affirming flame to the ironic points of
light he was charting on the world map, but he'd been to Germany in
1928 and 1945 and he was not naively optimistic:

> Napoleon was really the precursor of Hitler. The Germans,
> after you've said everything there is to say about the inflation,
> the depression, and the disorder, are really culpable for having
> chosen Hitler. They knew what they were getting in for. ... Hitler
> had to be smashed completely. That was the first job. But then
> you had immediately to help the enemy with all your strength.[41]

By 1950, Auden had aligned his work as poet with the less heroic,
more socially committed figure of a builder or maker who, among
many others, contributes to the communal post-war task of
reconstructing, stone by stone, the ruined walls of the city.[42] In Old
English, which Auden studied under J. R. R. Tolkien at Oxford, the
term for poet was *maker*.

Jung's critical psychology of type gave Auden a compass with
which to orient readers, each through his or her own Age of Anxiety. The
poem inspired other artists such as Bernstein, Robbins, Neumeier, and
Scarlett to bring and hold together hosts of disparate elements in rich
and open dialectics.[43] Likewise, Stossel locates himself at the border

between anxiety defined as a meaningful idiom of mental distress and a psychiatric mental disorder (whether genetically programmed or environmentally nurtured) that, unfortunately, neither medication nor cognitive therapy alleviates. Like Auden, Stossel depicts our culture as increasingly impoverished linguistically, the word *anxiety* losing its rich historical accumulation of philosophical and psychological connotations to a psychiatric denotation that is symptom-defined and market-imposed. Auden compensates for such impoverishment by mapping a complex cosmology in which he positions anxiety as a primary concern. Jung's multi-voiced psychology of type corroborates Auden's conviction about the relationship between anxiety and the dialectical nature of poetic truth.

NOTES

1. Jung qualified his taxonomy of psychological types. He also emphasized that theories need not be combined to form a "grand narrative." He wrote,

> Very many theories are needed before we can get even a rough picture of the psyche's complexity. It is therefore quite wrong when people accuse psychotherapists of being unable to reach agreement even on their own theories. Agreement could only spell one-sidedness and desiccation. One could as little catch the psyche in a theory as one could catch the world. Theories are not articles of faith, they are either instruments of knowledge and of therapy, or they are no good at all.

C. G. Jung, "Medicine and Psychotherapy" (1945), in *The Practice of Psychotherapy*, in *The Collected Works of C. G. Jung*, vol. 16, ed. and trans. Gerhard Adler and R. F. C. Hull (Princeton, NJ: Princeton University Press, 1954), § 198.

2. James Merrill, *Collected Prose*, quoted in Aidan Wasley, *The Age of Auden: Postwar Poetry and the American Scene* (Princeton, NJ: Princeton University Press, 2011), p. 99.

3. Jan Zwicky, "Auden as Philosopher: How Poets Think" (Ralph Gustafson Lecture, Vancouver Island University, Nanaimo, Oct. 20, 2011); and *Auden as Philosopher: How Poets Think* (Institute for Coastal Research, 2012), p. 20.

4. For Freud on primary processes, see Sigmund Freud, "The Unconscious" (1915), vol. XIV; *The Interpretation of Dreams* (1900), vol. V; "Beyond the Pleasure Principle" (1920), vol. XVIII;

"Formulations on the Two Principles of Mental Functioning" (1911), vol. XII; and "Project for a Scientific Psychology" (1895), vol. 1. For Auden, see W. H. Auden, "Making, Knowing, Judging"; see also "Phantasy and Reality in Poetry," in Katherine Bucknell and Nicholas Jenkins, eds., '*In Solitude, for Company': W. H. Auden after 1940* (Oxford: Clarendon Press, 1995), pp. 177–96.

5. See, for example, C. G. Jung, "Psychology and Literature," *The Spirit in Man, Art and Literature*, in *The Collected Works of C. G. Jung*, vol. 15, ed. and trans. Gerhard Adler and R. F. C. Hull, Bollingen Series (Princeton, NJ: Princeton University Press, 1950/1966), §§ 139–41.

> For the sake of clarity I would like to call the one mode of artistic creation psychological, and the other visionary. The psychological mode works with materials drawn from man's conscious life— with crucial experiences, powerful emotions, suffering, passion, the stuff of human fate in general. All this is assimilated by the psyche of the poet, raised from the commonplace to the level of poetic experience, and expressed with a power of conviction that gives us a greater depth of human insight by making us vividly aware of those everyday happenings which we tend to evade or overlook because we perceive them only dully or with a feeling of discomfort. ... Here [with the visionary modes of artistic creation] everything is reversed. The experience that furnishes the material for artistic expression is no longer familiar. It is something strange that derives its existence from the hinterland of man's mind, as if it had emerged from the abyss of prehumen ages, or from a superhuman world of contrasting light and darkness. It is a primordial experience which surpasses man's understanding and to which in his weakness he may easily succumb.

6. Andrew Samuels, Bani Shorter, and Fred Plaut, *A Critical Dictionary of Jungian Analysis* (London: Routledge and Kegan Paul, 1986), p. 25.

7. C. G. Jung, *Memories, Dreams, Reflections* (New York: Random House, 1962), p. 298.

8. C. G. Jung, "On *The Tibetan Book of the Great Liberation*," *Psychology and Religion: West and East*, in *The Collected Works of C. G. Jung*, vol. 11, ed. and trans. Gerhard Adler and R. F. C. Hull (Princeton, NJ: Princeton University Press, 1958), § 772.

9. "The Wandering Jew," *New Republic* (1941), in *The Collected Works of W. H. Auden*, prose, vol. 2, ed. Edward Mendelson (Princeton, NJ: Princeton University Press, 2002), pp. 112–13.

10. In a similar passage, Jung writes,

> I myself have known more than one person who owed his entire usefulness and reason for existence to a neurosis which prevented all the worst follies in his life and forced him to a mode of living that developed his valuable potentialities. These might have been stifled had not the neurosis, with iron grip, held him to the place where he belonged. There are actually people who have the whole meaning of their life, their true significance, in the unconscious, while in the conscious mind is nothing but inveiglement and error. With others the case is reversed, and here neurosis has a different meaning. In these cases, but not in the former, a thoroughgoing reduction is indicated.

C. G. Jung, "On the Psychology of the Unconscious," *Two Essays on Analytical Psychology*, in *The Collected Works of C. G. Jung*, vol. 7, ed. and trans. Gerhard Adler and R. F. C. Hull, Bollingen Series XX (Princeton, NJ: Princeton University Press, 1953/1966), § 68.

11. See, for example, Tom Sawyer, "The Shadow in the Garden: Auden's Jungian Quests," *ARIEL: A Review of International English Literature* 15 (1, 1984): 67-85; and Edward Callan, "Allegory in Auden's *The Age of Anxiety*," *Twentieth-Century Literature* 10 (4, 1965): 155–65.

Jungians are not the only guilty party in this respect. In a two-day conference on Arendt and Auden's *The Age of Anxiety*, Homi Bhabha and Susannah Gottlieb neither acknowledged Auden's reading of Jung nor mentioned the Jungian underpinnings of the poem, but they introduced Auden (who never read Lacan) into Lacanian theorizing. Listen to Homi Bhabha, "Poetics of Anxiety and Security: The Problem of Speech and Action in Our Time," conference, Apr. 27–28, 2012, Serpentine Gallery. Accessed Jun. 11, 2015, at http://backdoorbroadcasting.net/2012/04/poetics-of-anxiety-and-security-the-problem-of-speech-and-action-in-our-time-homi-bhabha-on-auden-and-arendt/.

12. Alan Jacobs, "Introduction," in W. H. Auden, *The Age of Anxiety*, ed. Alan Jacobs (Princeton, NJ: Princeton University Press, 2011), p. xxi.

13. "It would be interesting to know what fraction of those who begin reading it persist to the end." *Ibid.*, p. xi.

14. Edward Mendelson, "From Myth to Parable." Mendelson identifies this shift with Auden individuating from interpreting the body as symbolic to experiencing his own body consciously as

intimately Other, the body possessing significance by sheer virtue of existing; this occurs immediately after the completion of *The Age of Anxiety*. I would argue that, in terms of Jung's theory of types, it makes teleological sense for an Introverted Thinking-Intuitive type to begin to integrate experiences of introverted sensation. Perhaps this shift is prefigured in the poem itself, as I mentioned, when Auden identifies his work as baroque, that is to say, as deliberately theatricalizing materiality in order to counter a hegemony of rational discourse.

15. W. H. Auden, "The Public v. the Late Mr. William Butler Yeats," *Partisan Review*, Spring 1939, in Auden, *Collected Works*, vol. 2, p. 3.

16. Oliver Sacks knew Auden personally and describes him functioning with others precisely in such terms:

> He became a living mirror for me—someone who could detect and encourage the perception of new vistas, images, and trains-of-thought long before I myself was conscious of them. And if he did this with me, he did it with hundreds of others. He showed us ourselves, he drew us into greater possibilities of being—'self-actualization,' to use the current, trendy word—by being himself, wise and tolerant and affectionate as Socrates, completely devoid of censoriousness and moralizing, yet deeply, purely, and passionately ethical.

Oliver Sacks, in Stephen Spender, ed., *W. H. Auden: A Tribute* (New York: Macmillan, 1975), p. 191.

17. W. H. Auden, "Address on Henry James," delivered Oct. 24, 1946, *Gazette of the Grolier Club*, February 1947, in Auden, *Collected Works*, vol. 2, p. 300.

18. C. G. Jung, *On Psychological and Visionary Art: Notes on the Lecture on Gérard de Nerval*, ed. Craig Stephenson (Princeton, NJ: Princeton University Press, 2015).

19. C. G. Jung, "The Transcendent Function" (1916/1957), *The Structure and Dynamics of the Psyche*, in *The Collected Works of C. G. Jung*, vol. 8, ed. and trans. Gerhard Adler and R. F. C. Hull (Princeton, NJ: Princeton University Press, 1960), 67–91.

20. W. H. Auden, "The Rewards of Patience," in Auden, *Collected Works*, vol. 2, p. 156.

21. Similarly, as a jurist for the Bollingen Prize, Auden took a strong ethical position, defending the nominated work of Ezra Pound when the organizers of the prize were voicing their understandable

objections to Pound's politics and propagandistic rhetoric. Auden insisted upon the moral and aesthetic obligation to grant Pound the prize based on the merit of his superior poetic legacy and regardless of his life choices. See Nicolas Jenkins, "Auden in America," *The Cambridge Companion to W. H. Auden*, ed. Stan Smith (Cambridge: Cambridge University Press, 2004), pp. 39–54.

22. It is like the shift at the end of Edith Sitwell's poem, "Still falls the Rain— / Then—O Ile leape up to my God: who pulles me doune—," in Edith Sitwell, "Still Falls the Rain: The Raids, 1940, Night and Day" (1940), *Collected Poems* (London: Sinclair-Stevenson, 1993).

23. "The axis between the superior and the inferior functions is what I have called the 'spine' of personality." John Beebe, "Psychological Types," *The Handbook of Jungian Psychology*, ed. Renos Papadopoulos (London: Routledge, 2006), p. 140.

24. C. G. Jung wrote, "Logically, the opposite of love is hate, and of Eros, Phobos (fear); but psychologically, it is the will to power. Where love reigns, there is no will to power; and where the will to power is paramount, love is lacking." Jung, "On the Psychology of the Unconscious," CW 7, § 78.

25. Søren Kierkegaard, *The Concept of Anxiety: A Simple Psychologically Oriented Deliberation in View of the Dogmatic Problem of Hereditary Sin*, ed. and trans. Alastair Hannay (New York: Liveright Publishing, 2014), p. 187.

26. Reinhold Niebuhr, *The Nature and the Destiny of Man (1941/1943)* (Louisville, KY: Westminster John Know Press, 1996); and Paul Tillich, "Existential Philosophy," *Journal of the History of Ideas* 5 (1, 1944): 44–70.

27. "Anxiety Disorders," American Psychiatric Association, *Diagnostic and Statistical Manual of Mental Disorders*, Fifth Edition (Washington, DC: American Psychiatric Publishing, 2013), p. 190. In the latest edition of the *DSM*, "Posttraumatic Stress Disorder" has moved from "Anxiety Disorders" to "Trauma- and Stressor-Related Disorders"; see "Posttraumatic Stress Disorder, 309.81 (F.43.10)," in American Psychiatric Association, *Diagnostic and Statistical Manual of Mental Disorders*, Fifth Edition (Washington, DC: American Psychiatric Publishing, 2013), pp. 271–80.

28. In my opinion, the best is Martin Antony and Murray Stein, *The Oxford Handbook of Anxiety and Related Disorders* (Oxford: Oxford University Press, 2008). See also Martin Antony and Peter J. Norton,

The Anti-Anxiety Workbook: Proven Strategies to Overcome Worry, Phobias, Panic, and Obsessions (New York: Guildford Press, 2008).

29. In Peter Kramer, *Listening to Prozac: The Landmark Book about Antidepressants and the Remaking of the Self* (New York: Viking, 1993), p. 246, psychiatrist Peter Kramer wondered whether "cosmetic psychopharmacology" might be the wave of the future, whereby healthy people consume medication to remake their personalities so they can become "better than well"; and in his article "Psychotropic Hedonism vs. Pharmacological Calvinism" in *The Hastings Center Report* 2 (1972): pp. 1–3, G. L. Klerman coined the phrase *pharmacological Calvinism* to describe the rationale of denying drug treatment (or psychotherapy) to people suffering from genuine mental disorders. See Richard McNally, *What is Mental Illness?* (Cambridge, MA: Harvard University Press, 2011), p. 41.

30. "Generalized Anxiety Disorder," pp. 222–26.

31. In the Grimm's tale "Clever Elsie," the protagonist's so-called cleverness (i.e., her intuitive function) manifests negatively as a fear of future possibility, and her anxieties disorder the entire family:

> Then Clever Elsie took the pitcher from the wall, went into the cellar, and tapped the lid briskly as she went, so that the time might not appear long. When she was below she fetched herself a chair, and set it before the barrel so that she had no need to stoop, and did not hurt her back or do herself any unexpected injury. Then she placed the can before her, and turned the tap, and while the beer was running she would not let her eyes be idle, but looked up at the wall, and after much peering here and there, saw a pick-axe exactly above her, which the masons had accidentally left there.
>
> Then Clever Elsie began to weep and said: 'If I get Hans, and we have a child, and he grows big, and we send him into the cellar here to draw beer, then the pick-axe will fall on his head and kill him.' Then she sat and wept and screamed with all the strength of her body, over the misfortune which lay before her. Those upstairs waited for the drink, but Clever Elsie still did not come. Then the woman said to the servant: 'Just go down into the cellar and see where Elsie is.' The maid went and found her sitting in front of the barrel, screaming loudly. 'Elsie why do you weep?' asked the maid. 'Ah,' she answered, 'have I not reason to weep? If I get Hans, and we have a child, and he grows big, and has to draw beer here, the pick-axe will perhaps fall on his head, and kill him. 'Then said the maid: 'What a clever Elsie we

have!' And sat down beside her and began loudly to weep over the misfortune. After a while, as the maid did not come back, those upstairs were thirsty for the beer, the man said to the boy: 'Just go down into the cellar and see where Elsie and the girl are.' The boy went down, and there sat Clever Elsie and the girl both weeping together. Then he asked: 'Why are you weeping?' 'Ah,' said Elsie, 'have I not reason to weep? If I get Hans, and we have a child, and he grows big, and has to draw beer here, the pick-axe will fall on his head and kill him.' Then said the boy: 'What a clever Elsie we have!' And sat down by her, and likewise began to howl loudly. Upstairs they waited for the boy, but as he still did not return, the man said to the woman: 'Just go down into the cellar and see where Elsie is!' The woman went down, and found all three in the midst of their lamentations, and inquired what was the cause, then Elsie told her also that her future child was to be killed by the pick-axe, when it grew big and had to draw beer, and the pick-axe fell down. Then said the mother likewise: 'What a clever Elsie we have!' And sat down and wept with them. The man upstairs waited a short time, but as his wife did not come back and his thirst grew ever greater, he said: 'I must go into the cellar myself and see where Elsie is.' But when he got into the cellar, and they were all sitting together crying, and he heard the reason, and that Elsie's child was the cause, and that Elsie might perhaps bring one into the world some day, and that he might be killed by the pick-axe, if he should happen to be sitting beneath it, drawing beer just at the very time when it fell down, he cried: 'Oh, what a clever Elsie!' and sat down, and likewise wept with them.

32. Barry E. Wolfe, *Understanding and Treating Anxiety Disorders* (Washington, DC: American Psychiatric Publishing, 2005).

33. Scott Stossel, *My Age of Anxiety: Hope, Dread, and the Search for Peace of Mind* (New York: Knopf, 2014).

34. Homi Bhabha's important lecture addresses Auden's notion of poetic truth and its connection to Arendt's concepts of agency and author. Bhabha, "Poetics of Anxiety and Security. Accessed Jun. 11, 2015, at http://backdoorbroadcasting.net/2012/04/poetics-of-anxiety-and-security-the-problem-of-speech-and-action-in-our-time-homi-bhabha-on-auden-and-arendt/.

35. Auden, "Address on Henry James," p. 302.

36. Nicholas Jenkins, "Historical as Munich—Auden at 100: Who is he now?" *Times Literary Supplement*, Feb. 9, 2007, pp. 12–5.

37. W. H. Auden, "Psychology and Art Today," *The Arts Today* (1935), in *The Complete Works of W. H. Auden*, prose, vol. 1, ed. Edward Mendelson (Princeton, NJ: Princeton University Press, 1996), p. 100.

38. W. H. Auden, Notebook 1930, British Library Add. MS. 52430, in Humphrey Carpenter, *W. H. Auden: A Biography* (Boston, MA: Houghton Mifflin, 1981), p. 92.

39. W. H. Auden's poem, "The More Loving One," can be interpreted as an anterotic poem. See Craig E. Stephenson, *Anteros: A Forgotten Myth* (London: Routledge, 2013). Auden and Kallman collaborated on the libretto for Stravinsky's *The Rake's Progress*. According to Stravinsky's assistant Robert Craft, "the real subject of the libretto was the fidelity of true love." The Hero, Tom Rakewell, falls under the influence of a Jungian villain called Nick Shadow. Kallman wrote most of Anne Truelove's lines, while Auden composed most of the rake's, a reversal of their erotic roles in real life. Kallman later said he had found writing the libretto a task approaching penance. Carpenter, *W. H. Auden*, p. 354.

40. W. H. Auden, "In Praise of the Brothers Grimm," *The New York Times Book Review*, Nov. 12, 1944, in Auden, *Complete Works*, vol. 2, p. 242.

41. Alan Ansen, *The Table Talk of W. H. Auden*, ed. Nicholas Jenkins (Princeton, NJ: Ontario Review Press, 1990), pp. 30–1.

42. See W. H. Auden, *The Enchafèd Flood: Or the Romantic Iconography of the Sea*, in *The Complete Works of W. H. Auden*, prose, vol. 3, ed. Edward Mendelson (Princeton, NJ: Princeton University Press, 2008), pp. 1–94.

43. "Someday it will have to be told how Jungianism, which started out in US Art more or less as anti-Fascist psychoanalytic modernism, turned into the analysis of patriarchy and thereby cleared the way for what was to come." Mark Franko, *Martha Graham in Love and War: The Life in the Work* (Oxford: Oxford University Press, 2012), p. 177.

Figure 1: Berserkers, The Lewis Chessman, courtesy of the British Museum, London.

APPENDIX

AN ARCHETYPAL MAPPING OF A SOLDIER'S POST-WAR ANXIETY IN GRIMM'S "BEARSKIN"

In a 1945 lecture, Jung used fairy tales to provide images of how individuals, leaders, and entire societies suffer possession by destructive unconscious complexes. Jung depicted enlightened rationalists pointing proudly

> to the advances in physics and medicine, to the freeing of the mind from medieval stupidity and—as a well-meaning Christian—to our deliverance from the fear of demons. But we continue to ask: what have all our other cultural achievements led to? ... Can we not understand that all the outward tinkerings and improvements do not touch man's inner nature, and that everything ultimately depends upon whether the man who wields the science and the technics is capable of responsibility or not?[1]

Referring to the outcome of two world wars and the prospect of nuclear annihilation, Jung contrasted the technical advancements of twentieth-century humans, with their lack of psychological sophistication, and the impoverishment of their symbolic lives. For similar reasons, in 1944 Auden recommended the reading of *Grimm's Fairy Tales* as a "must" for every post-war adult: "among the few indispensable, common-property books upon which Western culture can be founded ... it is hardly too much to say that the tales rank next to the Bible in importance."[2]

The Grimm brothers called their many folk-tale collections *Kinder und Hausmärchen* (*Children's and Household Tales*); *Grimm's Fairy Tales* is the less appropriate title in English. In these books, there are ten stories about soldiers and wartime: "The Three Snake Leaves," "How Six Made Their Way in the World," "Brother Lustig," "The Devil's Sooty Brother," "Bearskin," "The Blue Light," "The Devil and His Grandmother," "The Shoes That Were Danced to Pieces," "The Grave Mound," and "The Boots of Buffalo Leather." The sources of these tales varied greatly: from Johann Friedrich Krause, a former soldier, and Dorothea Viehmann, a peasant woman, to literary works published by Friedmund von Arnim. In the historical context of these tales, common soldiers were dissatisfied with their treatment by their superiors. Their lot was miserable. As members of a standing army, they had few rights and underwent long periods of strict drilling. Corporal punishment was the rule for many offenses. They were hated by both peasants and town dwellers, who were obliged to house them and pay for their maintenance. If Grimm's soldiers are characterized as fearless, it is often because, in real life, soldiers had little to lose.

We know that politically the Grimm brothers believed in social mobility and respect for a person's qualities, regardless of class or trade. As time passed, their sentiments against class distinctions grew more radical. This democratic sensibility is imbedded in both the setting of the forest and the movement of the soldiers' stories towards a new sense of social justice. In the forest of one of the tales, a discharged soldier full of rage finds five extraordinary companions who help him gain vengeance on the king. In the forest of another tale, a discharged soldier meets the devil, who will enable him to procure money and marry well; or, in another, he meets a witch, through whom he finds the blue light with which he will punish the king and marry his daughter. In this particular story, the Grimms revised their sentences to heighten the sense of injustice. Only in "The Three Snake Leaves" is the soldier actually enlisted rather than discharged. He goes forth to fight for the fatherland, but he is murdered by the king's daughter and gains justice through the magic of the snake leaves. So, all these common soldiers in Grimm's tales are forced to be fearless, opportunistic, and ambitious. With his knapsack, Brother Lustig even tricks his way into Heaven. For the Grimms, these soldiers' stories are compensatory narratives, in which the soldiers gain revenge by aligning themselves temporarily with the devil. They possess a simple kind of integrity, but, to the extent that revenge drives these stories forward, love and compassion cannot be at their center. These soldiers may help people and animals, but they are out to prove and empower themselves. They are underprivileged men who need to display the right civil sense of cunning to make their way back into society.

The story "Bearskin" proves to be the exception to the rule. In the first four editions of their tales, the Grimms included "The Devil's Greenjacket," a story about a foolish young man who squanders his inheritance. He makes a bargain with the devil. He will wear the devil's waistcoat, whose pockets are always full of money, on condition that he not wash, trim his hair and nails, or pray for seven years; if he does, he will lose his soul. But for the fifth edition of their book (1843), they rewrote the story, combining it with details from a story by Hans Jakob Christoffel von Grimmelshausen, "Der erste Bärenhäuter" ("The First Bearskinner") (1670). They turned the foolish young protagonist who accepts the devil's ordeal into a soldier back from the war, and they changed the title of their story to "Bearskin." The story addresses the psychological suffering of soldiers after active service in combat. Changing the protagonist from a young man abandoned by his two older brothers after the death of their father, to a soldier returning from war, the Grimms spoke to two questions of soldiering in their time: how to integrate a warring—Auden would say, an eristic—spirit during peacetime, and how to heal the anxiety and loss of self that comes with leaving one's comrades and returning home from combat. A narrative analysis of "Bearskin" makes explicit the psychological map with which the Grimms wanted every household to be familiar, a description of a soldier's process of intrapsychically recovering self and interpersonally reconnecting to society.

The Grimms refined this story for the definitive seventh edition of their tales (1857). A story that today is not well-known,[3] "Bearskin" describes an apparently fearless soldier who returns from war to find himself without work (it is peacetime and he only knows how to shoot) and without a home (his parents have died and his hard-hearted brothers have forsaken him). Why did they give so much attention to this story?

Dedicated to democratizing the princely German states and forging a common cultural identity for their society, the Brothers Grimm also published dictionaries of the German language. In Volume 1 of their *Deutsches Wörterbuch* (1852), they define the term "Bärenhäuter" (bearskinner) as an ambiguous word, often used to reprimand someone as a layabout. But they point out that the word may also have had a positive connotation and cite Grimmelshausen, the fifteenth-century chronicler of the Thirty Years War (Otto, 2010).[4] The story the Grimms borrow from Grimmelshausen for their collection tells of an event that happened in 1396, when the Ottoman emperor invaded Hungary. A soldier escapes from a battle, kills a bear, and wears the skin as a coat, lingering in this half-animal, half-human state until finally he sheds the skin, bathes in the Rhine, and makes his way successfully back into society.

The Brothers Grimm combined Grimmelshausen's story with a traditional folktale. Their new version tells of a soldier who returns from a war and, now jobless, falls into anxiety and despair and finds himself bargaining for his life with a cloven-hoofed trickster. The soldier puts on the devil's green jacket, since the coat will provide him with money during the seven-year trial, and over the green

So fah ich aus/ich erster Beeren-
häuter
Den Nahmen ich bekam vons
Beeren-Haut
Den ich erschoß/daß mir nicht
einmal graut
Ob ich bekam gleich dazumal
viel Kleider.
So hoch mein Ruhm vor Zeiten
war gestiegen
So tieff muß er im höchsten
Schimpff jetzt liegen
Man sieht hieraus/was hochge-
acht wird heut
Das stürtzt der Neid in allzu-
kurtzer Zeit.

f. Prorurſicutius.

Figure 2: Hans Jacob Christoffel von Grimmelshausen, *Der erste Beernhäuter*, illustrated by Marcus Behmer, Berlin, Otto von Holten, Brandus'sche Verlagsbuchhandlung, 1919.

jacket he places the bearskin as the heavy cloak he must carry on his back and as the bed on which he must lie. This layering does more than accentuate the stipulations of not washing, not cutting his hair and nails, and not saying the Lord's Prayer for seven years. Taking their cue from Grimmelshausen, the Grimms emphasize the soldier's change of identity when the trickster spirit re-names him: "You shall be called Bearskin." The revised story becomes the chronicle of the test of endurance that the protagonist must undergo to re-enter human society.

By drawing attention to this stacking of clothing and layering of narratives, the Brothers Grimm pull their readers back through time, from the 1800s and the Napoleonic Wars (1803–1815) of their own day, to Grimmelshausen and the Thirty Years War (1618–1648), and even further back to 1396 and the Ottoman invasion that Grimmelshausen employs as the setting for his own soldier's story. And taking up Grimmelshausen's example, the Grimms use their narrative to account for the etymology of the hero's name and to reconnect readers with the images imbedded in common words. Jacob Grimm knew that the old Norse language possessed two compound nouns, *berserker* (bear shirt) and *úlfhedinn* (wolf coat), to describe certain warriors who reputedly entered battle screaming and biting the rims of their shields.[5] These warriors fought in a frenzied state, vanquished foes without being injured, and then fell into deep sleep. They were as strong as bears, as crazed as wolves, and they had the power to render their enemies blind, deaf, or witless from fear. The early medieval chess pieces now known as the Lewis Chessmen in the collection of the British Museum corroborate the prevalence of this lore. Made in Norway around 1150, found in 1831 on the Isle of Lewis in the outer Hebrides, three of the warders or rooks in the ancient chess set are berserkers, recognizable because they are biting their shields (See Figure 1).

In the Norse sagas, berserkers raped and murdered at will and were often portrayed as villains. For example, in the *Egils Saga Skallagrimssonar* attributed to Snorri Sturluson (1179–1241), the protagonist Egil narrates three generations, beginning in a pre-Christian pagan Norway, and gives a startling account of his grandfather, who, after life as a berserker, retired quietly to his farm.[6] Egil explains that when evening came, the old man would often become short of temper (become *styggr*, which means *wary* when applied to animals) and fall into a doze, during which he was vulnerable to uncontrolled *hamrammr* (shape-shifting). Also in the Völsunga saga, a father and son roam the forests, killing men for plunder to avenge wrongs done to the Völsungs by King Siggeir. When they chance upon a pair of wolf skins and decide to wear them, they fall into fighting and killing again, but without motive, and their transformation into wolves becomes a kind of curse that they cannot control.[7]

Clearly, the Grimms named their soldier "Bearskin" in allusion to these berserkers. Indeed, berserkers existed not just in legend but also in recorded history, having served as the household guard of King Harald the Fair-haired who first forged a unified Norwegian state by ruthlessly subjecting several independent kingdoms to his authority, AD 872–930. Jacob Grimm devoted an entire chapter of the second volume of his *Deutsche Mythologie* to tracing the theriomorphic notion of man-animal transformations in German mythology back to these Icelandic stories. It is not difficult to extrapolate from "soldiers who went forth to combat, raging like wolves, biting their shields, in strength equal to furious bears ... [fighting in a] frenzy known as *Berserksgangr*/rage," forward to the later medieval lore of lycanthropy or werewolves, of humans gripped unawares by destructive states of mind.[8]

In the twentieth century, psychoanalyst Bruno Bettelheim classified the theriomorphic element in such tales as the psychological struggle to humanize the Freudian id.[9] Jung emphasized that, without a strong psychotherapeutic container or frame, attempts to abreact or purge soldiers of difficult feeling-states were dangerous; he compared the terrible psychological wounding that an individual soldier might suffer in a personal confrontation with the archetypal spirit of war to the biblical Jacob's dark night of the soul, wrestling with a terrifying angel.[10] Only after the Vietnam War did the American Psychiatric Association introduce into its diagnostic manual the term Post-Traumatic Stress Disorder to identify what psychiatrists of previous wars had often labeled "shell shock" and "male hysteria." Veterans now prefer the neurological diagnosis of "brain trauma" that denotes a "real" rather than "phantom"-like wound.

In "Bearskin," the soldier confronts what Grimmelshausen calls a "spirit" and what the Grimms call the "Devil." First, the supernatural spirit tests that the soldier is indeed fearless, admonishing the young man to "look behind." As if out of nowhere, a bear attacks, which the soldier shoots, clearly by reflex. The Grimms' dictionary work would suggest that this bear is itself the theriomorphic expression of the spirit of war.[11] So the soldier kills the totemic animal-form of his own berserker/soldiering identity, and the spirit subjects him to wearing the carcass for seven years. What in wartime was his power and his pride is now in peacetime something that alienates him from the human society he served so fearlessly. Wherever he goes, people flee him, repulsed by his identification with the bearskin.

Figure 3: "Bearskin," in Grimm's *Household Tales*, translated by Marian Edwardes, illustrated by Robert Anning Bell, New York, Dutton, 1912, p. 87. New York Public Library. https://archive.org/details/grimmshouseholdt00grim.

The Grimm brothers' revised tale speaks to a two-sided problem in their time. There is the problem of the fearlessness of the soldier, of what to make of a wild warring spirit in peacetime, and there is the concomitant shadow problem of his brothers' "hardheartedness"; when the soldier asks to come home, they answer, "You, soldier, are of no use to us; go and make a living for yourself." The problem inherent in the heroic protagonist's psyche shifts in the nadir of the fourth of his seven years of endurance, when he hears the sound of a bankrupted old man weeping, opens a door to him, and feels empathy; however, even more important, the society to which the soldier has returned, the Brothers Grimm emphasize, remains hard-hearted.[12]

In the context of war, the soldier has risked his life and survived, but as if he is unconsciously possessed by the spirit of war, alternating like a berserker between periods of inflated fury and comatose spentness. Now, in peacetime, he risks losing his soul, because he can no longer swing back and forth between these two poles unawares but must endure consciously the inflation and deflation of being both a fearless war hero and a homeless vagrant. The Grimms configure the return to society as a necessarily unheroic seven-year rite of passage: slowly building a self that is strong enough to bear itself, to endure the truth about itself, to carry that truth on the back, and to lie in the bed of that one-sidedness of self that was also the soldier's heroic ideal, his fearlessness under fire.[13]

What sustains the individual in such a psychological process? Curiously enough, it is not only the green coat that pays the bills for seven years. Just as important is the framework or community that the soldier constructs around him by asking the poor he encounters to pray for him because he is not permitted to pray. And when he meets one of the bankrupted father's three daughters, he breaks a ring in two, giving her one half and keeping the other for himself. He continues on his journey for another three years, but now with the fragile hope that, both inwardly and outwardly, things may reconnect by the end of the seventh year. No doubt, the Grimms knew the etymology of the Greek word *symbolon*, which literally means to break an object in two in order to make a transaction with another person, the transaction being completed when they meet again and put the two pieces together. In other words, by the end of the seven years, the soldier uses a symbol to reconnect intrapsychically the opposing parts of his self, as well as to reconnect interpersonally as a member of his society.[14] In order to come through, he requires a symbolic life.

A narrative analysis of "Bearskin" makes explicit the psychological map the Grimms drew to introduce as fundamental cultural knowledge into their society. They created a symbolic story, at once new and yet timeworn, about how soldiers returning from active service must suffer through long and difficult transformations in order to reintegrate. An ethical as opposed to a hard-hearted society, knowing this story, would commit itself to assisting better those who served it during a time of war.

NOTES

1. C. G. Jung, "The Phenomenology of the Spirit in Fairy Tales" (1945), *The Archetypes and the Collective Unconscious*, in *The Collected Works of C. G. Jung*, vol. 9i, ed. and trans. Gerhard Adler and R. F. C. Hull (Princeton, NJ: Princeton University Press, 1959/1980), § 455.

2. W. H. Auden, "In Praise of the Brothers Grimm," *The New York Times Book Review*, Nov. 12, 1944, in *The Complete Works of W. H. Auden*, prose, vol. 2, ed. Edward Mendelson (Princeton, NJ: Princeton University Press, 2002), p. 240.

3. Jacob Grimm and Wilhelm Grimm, "Bearskin," in *The Complete Grimm's Fairy Tales* (London: Routledge and Kegan Paul, 1975), pp. 467–72.

4. K. F. Otto, ed., *A Companion to the Works of Grimmelshausen* (New York: Camden House, 2010).

5. J. Cathey, "Berserks," in *The Dictionary of the Middle Ages*, vol. 2, ed. J. R. Strayer (New York: Charles Scribner's Sons, 1983), p. 198.

6. *Egil's Saga*, trans. H. Pálsson and P. Edwards (Harmondsworth: Penguin, 1976).

7. Peter Orton, "Theriomorphism: Jacob Grimm, Old Norse Mythology, German Fairy Tales, and English Folklore, in *The Shadow-Walkers: Jacob Grimm's Mythology of the Monstrous*, ed. Tom Shippey (Tempe: Arizona State University Press, 2005), pp. 299–334.

8. Heimskringla, quoted in J. Robinson, *The Lewis Chessmen* (*Objects in Focus*) (London: British Museum Press; 2004), p. 26.

9. Bruno Bettelheim, *The Uses of Enchantment: The Meaning and Importance of Fairy Tales* (New York: Vintage, 1977/2010).

10. Jung, "The Phenomenology of the Spirit in Fairy Tales," CW 9i, §§ 207–54; Roger Brooke, "An Archetypal Perspective for Combat Trauma," *Bulletin of the American Academy of Clinical Psychology* 13 (1, 2012): 2–6; and R. Wyatt, E. Goodwyn, and M. Ignatowski, "A Jungian Approach to Dreams Reported by Soldiers in a Modern Combat Zone," in *Journal of Analytical Psychology* 56 (2, 2011): 217–31.

11. Michel Pastoureau, *The Bear: History of a Fallen King*, trans. George Holoch (Cambridge, MA: Harvard University Press, 2011).

12. Nicolas Kristof, "Veterans and Brain Disease," in *The New York Times*, Apr. 25, 2012; "War Wounds," in *The New York Times*, Aug. 10, 2012.

13. Jonathan Shay, *Achilles in Vietnam: Combat Trauma and the Undoing of Character* (New York: Scribner, 1994); *Odysseus in America: Combat Trauma and the Trials of Homecoming* (New York: Scribner, 2002).

14. Paul Lerner, *Hysterical Men: War, Psychiatry, and the Politics of Trauma in Germany, 1890–1930* (Ithaca, NY: Cornell University Press, 2003).

INDEX

A

Age of Anxiety, The (Auden):
  aesthetic evaluation of, 3–4
  baroque eclogue, 62
  Bernstein's response to, 1,
    76–86
  cosmology in, 114, 116, 117
  critical assessments of, 1,
    107, 108
  death camps reported in, 58
  epigraph of, 62–63
  Epilogue, 58–59
  first edition of, 60–61
  four protagonists of, 53–54
  initial work on, 24, 29
  inspiration for artists, 1, 116–117
  intrapsychic process depicted in,
    106–107
  Jacob's introduction to, 3, 49–
    50, 56, 58, 59
  Jungian influence in, 2
  meaning of anxiety addressed
    in, 109
  narrator, 53, 54, 55, 63
  Neumeier's choreography, 1,
    90–91, 106–107
  Prologue, 52, 80
  reception of, 75–76
  Robbins' choreography, 1,
    87–90, 106–107
  Scarlett's choreography, 1,
    91–96, 106–107
  setting of, 52
  structure of, 52–53
  temenos in, 51, 63
  writing of, 7–8, 30, 51,
  See also Protagonists,
    Symphony No. 2, Typology

"Age of Ice" (Auden), 42
"Ain't Got No Tears Left"
  (Bernstein), 82
All Souls Day, 52, 62
American Psychiatric Association
  (APA), 4, 110, 132
"Annunciation, The" (Auden), 44
Anxiety:
  Auden's questions about, 4
  diagnostic categories for, 4,
    110–112
  literary works about, 111–112
  meaning of, 109–110
  memoirs about, 108, 111–113
  psychoanalytic definition,
    110–111
  roots of, 105
  seen in "Bearskin", 129–134
Arbogast, Robert, 91
"Art of Healing, The" (Auden), 10
As You Like It (Shakespeare), 53–54
Ascent of F6 (Auden and
  Isherwood), 42
Atwood, Margaret, 84
"Auden as Philosopher"
  (Zwicky), 104
Auden, Bernard, 10
Auden, Constance Rosalie Bicknell,
  10–11, 14
Auden, George Augustus, 9–10,
  11, 13
Auden, John, 10, 12, 13
Auden, W. H.:
  birth of, 10
  childhood of, 11–12, 44–45
  commentary on *Tempest,* 27–28
  criticism of Freudian
    psychoanalysis, 105–106

departs to China, 18, 19
dislikes Bernstein's and
    Robbins' adaptations, 90
distrust of "September 1, 1939",
    8, 23, 24, 107
dream quest narrative by, 54–55
father of, 6, 9–10, 13
function of poetry, 8, 23, 24–25,
    28–29
influences in "New Year
    Letter", 25–27
intimacy with Jaffe, 51–52, 114
intuition and thinking function
    of, 44, 45, 46, 61–62, 84
Jung's influence on, 1–2, 41–43,
    49–50, 103–104, 110
Kierkegaard's influence on, 50
knowledge of, 41
leaves England, 21–22
letters to Ayerst, 3
marriage to Mann, 16–17
mother of, 10–11
move to America, 113
photos, 6, 19, 40, 46, 52, 74
poetic aspirations of, 107–108
problem of collective shadow,
    48–49
recommends *Grimm's Fairy
    Tales,* 114, 127
reconciling personal integrity, 22
relationship with Kallman,
    46–49, 50, 114
sexuality of, 13–14
social commitment of, 8–9, 116
study of Freud, 10, 14, 25, 41,
    105–106, 110
support of Spanish Civil War,
    17–18
swimming accident, 45
U.S. military service, 29–30
use of baroque eclogue, 62
use of typology, 43–44, 103–
    104, 107

war poems of, 24–25, 108
war's influence on, 7–8, 12
    See also Age of Anxiety, The
Aurélia (Nerval), 108
Ayerst, David, 13

B
"Ballade" (Robbins), 89
Barzun, Jacques, 75
Bateson, Gregory, 11
Beard, Dick, 88
"Bearskin" (Grimm brothers), 129–
    131, 132–134
Behold, This Dreamer (de la
    Mare), 42
Bernstein, Burton, 79
Bernstein, Leonard:
    begins Symphony No. 2, 79–80
    dispute with Robbins, 86, 90
    musical sketch for *Age of
        Anxiety,* 77
    photo of, 74
    portraying Rosetta's
        soliloquy, 110
    premieres Symphony No. 2,
        81, 83
    tone poem suggested to, 76–77
    use of typology, 78–79, 84–
        85, 116,
    See also Symphony No. 2
Berserkers, 131–134
Bettelheim, Bruno, 132
Black Books, The (Jung), 109
Blake, William, 12, 25, 44
Blanche, Dr. Émile, 113
"Blue Light, The" (Grimm
    brothers), 128
Bolender, Todd, 87, 88
"Boots of Buffalo Leather, The"
    (Grimm brothers), 128
Boston Symphony Orchestra, 83
Boultenhouse, Charles, 89–90
"Bride in the 30s, A" (Auden), 46

Britten, Benjamin, 43
"Brother Lustig" (Grimm brothers), 128
Brothers Grimm. *See Grimm's Fairy Tales*

C

Callan, Edgar, 2
"Cave of Making, The" (Auden), 28
Chicago Sun, The, 28–29
Childhood of Auden, 11–12, 44–45
Choreography for *The Age of Anxiety*:
    Jung's influence on, 2
    Neumeier, 1, 90–91, 106–107
    progression of emotion via, 106–107
    Robbins, 1, 87–90, 106–107
    Scarlett, 1, 91–96, 106–107,
    See also Symphony No. 2
Churchill, Winston, 46
Coghill, Nevill, 14, 107
Coleridge, Samuel, 104
Collected Poems (Auden), 8, 23, 84
Collected Works (Auden), 2–3, 107
"Commentary" (*Journey to a War*) (Auden), 20
Copland, Aaron, 78, 84
Cosmology of Auden, 113–116, 117

D

Dance. *See* Choreography for *The Age of Anxiety*
Dante, 25, 41, 52, 54
Davenport-Hines, Richard, 23–24
Davidson, Michael, 9
De la Mare, Walter, 42
De Rougemont, Denis, 43
"Democracy's Reply to the Challenge of Dictators" (Auden), 21
Der erste Beernhäuter (Grimmelshausen), 129, 130
Deutsche Mythologie (Grimm), 132

Deutsches Wörterbuch (Grimm brothers), 130
"Devil and His Grandmother, The" (Grimm brothers), 128
"Devil's Greenjacket, The" (Grimm brothers), 129
"Devil's Sooty Brother, The" (Grimm brothers), 128
Diagnostic and Statistical Manual of Mental Disorders (DSM), 4, 110–112
Dies Irae, 62
"Dirge, The" (*The Age of Anxiety*):
    Auden's work, 52, 56–57
    Bernstein's interpretation of, 80, 81–82
    Robbins' choreography of, 87–88
    Scarlett's choreography of, 94–95
Divine Comedy (Dante), 25, 52, 54
Dodds, A. E., 22
Dodds, E. R., 17, 23
Double bind, 11
Dreams, 54–55, 59
DSM (Diagnostic and Statistical Manual of Mental Disorders), 4, 110–112
Dunning, Jennifer, 90
Dyer, Tristan, 93

E

Early Auden (Mendelson), 2
Eclogue, 62
Edwardes, Marian, 133
Egils Saga Skallagrimssonar (Sturluson), 131
Emble, 53, 55, 57, 93, 95
English National Ballet, 92
"Epilogue" (*The Age of Anxiety*):
    Scarlett's choreography of, 95
    Symphony No. 2 (Bernstein), 83, 84

"Eros and Agape" (Auden), 43
Essay on Man (Pope), 26
Exploring the Unconscious
 (Groddeck), 43
Extroverted Feeling type, 84–85

F

Facsimile (Bernstein/Robbins), 86
Fairy tales, Jung's use of, 127
"Family Ghosts" (Auden), 41–42
Fancy Free (Bernstein/Robbins), 86
Fantasia of the Unconscious
 (Lawrence), 14
Faust (Goethe), 26
Feeling (Rosetta), 53, 54, 55, 56,
 57–58, 59, 61, 82, 83, 84, 93, 95,
 96, 106–107, 109–110
Feeling-Sensation type, 44
Folk tales about war, 128–134
For the Time Being (Auden), 27, 44,
 50, 107
Forster, E. M., 18, 27
Foss, Lukas, 83
Frankl, Viktor, 110
Freud, Sigmund, 43
 Auden's study of, 10, 14, 25,
 41, 105–106, 110
 Groddeck's influence on, 14
 identifies root of anxiety, 105
Fuller, John, 2, 41, 42, 60, 107

G

Gartside, Bennet, 93
Generalized anxiety, 111
Goethe, Johann Wolfgang, 12, 26, 54
"Grave Mound, The" (Grimm
 brothers), 128
Grimm brothers. *See Grimm's
 Fairy Tales*
Grimm, Jacob, 132
Grimmelshausen, Hans Jacob
 Christoffel, 129, 130–131, 132

Grimm's Fairy Tales:
 Auden recommends, 114, 127
 "Bearskin", 129–131, 132–134
 war stories in, 128
Groddeck, Georg, 14–15, 41, 42, 43
Guardian, The, 86

H

Harald the Fair-haired, 132
Hardy, Thomas, 25, 41, 44–45
Harper's Magazine, 75
Henk, Emil, 30
Hitler, Adolf, 46
*Homer Lane Talks to Parents and
 Teachers* (Lane), 14
Hopper, Edward, 93
Household Tales (Grimm, trans. by
 Edwardes), 133
"How Six Made Their Way in the
 World" (Grimm brothers), 128
Howard's End (Forster), 18
Huff, Sarah Wallin, 84

I

Imagination, 104–105
"In Memory of Ernst Toller"
 (Auden), 42
"In Time of War" (Auden), 18, 42
Inferior function, 47
Instinct and the Unconscious
 (Rivers), 9
Introverted Thinking type, 110
Introverted Thinking-Intuitive type,
 44, 45, 61–62, 84, 114
Introverted Thinking-Sensation type,
 47–48
Intuition (Quant), 53, 54, 55, 57, 58,
 81, 93, 95
Isherwood, Chester:
 Ascent of F6, 42
 collaborations with Auden, 7,
 11–12

friendship with Auden, 13, 46
photos, 19
publishes *Journey to a War,*
18–20, 42, 58
travels to United States,
21–22, 24

J

Jacobs, Alan, 3, 49–50, 56, 58, 59,
62, 107
Jaffe, Rhoda, 51–52, 114
James, Henry, 13, 108
Jenkins, Nicholas, 113
Jerusalem (Blake), 25
Journey to a War (Auden and
Isherwood), 18–20, 42, 58
Jowitt, Deborah, 86
Jung, Carl Gustav:
clients' need for self-expression,
108–109
identifying roots of anxiety, 105
influence on Auden, 1–2, 41–
43, 49–50, 103–104, 110
Mendelson's views on, 2–3
on problem of collective
shadow, 48–49
on typology theory, 56, 61, 107
use of fairy tales, 127,
See also Typology

K

Kallman, Chester, 7, 43, 46–49, 50,
51, 114
Kierkegaard, Søren:
on anxiety, 110
Auden's study of, 28, 41
interpretation of love, 50
Kinder und Hausmärchen. See
Grimm's Fairy Tales
Kipling, Rudyard, 25
Kirstein, Lincoln, 90
Kodat, Catherine Gunther, 3

Koussevitzky, Serge Alexandrovich,
77, 80, 83
Krause, Johann Friedrich, 128

L

Lane, Homer, 14–15, 41, 114
Langland, William, 41, 54, 62
Later Auden (Mendelson), 2
Lawrence, D. H., 14–15, 41, 114
Lawrence, Frieda, 79
Layard, John, 14, 43
Le Clercq, Tanaquil, 87, 88
"Letter to Lord Byron" (Auden), 11
"Literary Transference, A" (Auden),
44–45
Literary works:
Auden's cosmology in, 113–
116, 117
expanding themes of *Age of
Anxiety,* 106–107
folk tales about war, 128–134
inspired by typology, 106,
116–117
linking Life to, 109
memoirs, 108, 111–113,
See also Poetry *and specific
works by Auden*
Love in the Western World (de
Rougemont), 43
Lynes, George Platt, 87, 88

M

Macfarlane, John, 92–93
Malin, 53, 55, 56, 57, 58–59, 61, 81,
83, 84, 86, 93, 95–96, 109
Man and His Symbols (Jung), 90
Mann, Erika, 16–17
Man's Search for Meaning
(Frankl), 110
Marriage:
Auden's to Mann, 16–17

shadow within, 43
Martin, John, 88–89
Marx, Karl, 25, 41
"Masque, The" (*The Age of Anxiety*):
    Auden's writing of, 52, 57
    Bernstein's interpretation of, 80,
        81–83
    Robbins' choreography of, 88
    Scarlett's choreography of, 95
Maxwell, Glyn, 85–86
May, Rollo, 110
Mayer, Elizabeth, 24
McRae, Steven, 93
Meaning of Anxiety, The (May), 110
Medley, Robert, 12
Memoirs, 108, 111–113
Mendelson, Edward, 2–3, 13, 17, 18,
    20, 21, 26, 107, 115
Merrill, James, 104
Military service of Auden, 29–30
Morera, Laura, 93
Morris, Marketa, 78, 79
Music. *See* Symphony No. 2
    (Bernstein)
Mussolini, Benito, 46
My Age of Anxiety (Stossel), 1,
    112–113

N

Napoleonic Wars, 131
Narrator, 53, 54, 55, 63
Nerval, Gérard de, 108, 113
Neumeier, John:
    choreography by, 1, 90–91,
        106–107
    photos, 91
    portraying Rosetta's
        soliloquy, 110
    typology in, 116
Neurosis, 111
"New Year Letter" (Auden), 24,
    26–27, 50

New York Herald Tribune, The, 89
New York Times, The, 88–89, 114, 116
New Yorker, The, 42
Niebuhr, Reinhold, 41, 110
"Nighthawks" (Hopper), 93
Nijinsky, Vaslav, 23
"1929" (Auden), 15
"No Man's Land" (Scarlett), 91–92
Noll, Renée, 78–79

O

"O Tell Me the Truth about Love"
    (Auden), 46
O'Brien, Shaun, 88
"On Psychical Energy" (Jung), 41
On the Town (Bernstein), 82
Opera libretti by Auden, 7, 43–44
"Opera on an American Legend"
    (Auden), 43
Orwell, George, 17–18
Out of Revolution (Rosenstock-
    Huessy), 62

P

Paid on Both Sides: A Charade
    (Auden), 9
Partisan Review, 75
Paul Bunyan (Britten and Auden),
    43–44
Payne, Kristopher, 91
"Perfectly Subjective" (Auden),
    57–58
Perrault, Charles, 54
"Phenomenology of the Spirit in
    Fairy Tales, The" (Jung), 43
Piers Plowman (Langland), 41, 54, 62
Plaut, Fred, 105
Poetry:
    Auden's view of, 15–16, 104
    Auden's war, 24–25, 108
    dream quest narrative, 54–55
    eclogue, 62
    formalism in, 104

function of, 8, 23, 24–25, 28–29
qualities of great poets, 107–108
social commitment in Auden's,
    8–9, 116
as way out of psychosis, 108,
    See also Age of Anxiety, The
"Poetry, Poets, and Taste"
    (Auden), 16
Pope, Alexander, 26, 41
Post-Traumatic Stress Disorder
    (PTSD), 4, 132
Pound, Ezra, 89
"Preface to Kierkegaard, A"
    (Auden), 50
Problem of Anxiety, The (Freud), 110
Prolific and the Devourer, The
    (Auden), 24
"Prologue" (*The Age of Anxiety*),
    52, 80
Protagonists for *The Age of Anxiety*:
    Emble, 53, 55, 57, 93, 95
    Malin, 53, 55, 56, 57, 58–59,
        61, 81, 83, 86, 93,
        95–96, 109
    Quant, 53, 54, 55, 58, 81, 93, 95
    Rosetta, 53, 54, 55, 56, 57–58,
        59, 61, 82, 83, 84, 93, 95,
        106–107, 109–110
Psychoanalysis:
    Auden's rejection of orthodox,
        49–50
    Auden's study of Freudian, 10,
        14, 25, 41, 105–106, 110
    Bernstein's participation in, 78
    client self-expression in,
        108–109
    defining anxiety, 110–111
Psychological Types (Jung), 2, 3,
    61, 90
"Psychology and Art Today"
    (Auden), 42, 113

Psychology of the Unconscious
    (Jung), 42
Psychoneurosis, 110–111
"Public v. the Late Mr. William
    Butler Yeats, The" (Auden), 107
Pudney, John, 12

Q

Quant, 53, 54, 55, 58, 81, 93, 95

R

Red Book, The (Jung), 109, 113
Rilke, Rainer Maria, 25
Rimbaud, Arthur, 25
Rivers, W. H. R., 9, 20
Robbins, Jerome:
    choreography by, 1, 87–90,
        106–107
    dispute with Bernstein, 86, 90
    photos, 87, 88
    portraying Rosetta's
        soliloquy, 110
    typology in, 116
Rogers, Jeffrey, 91
Romanticism, 12, 48–49
Romney, Richard Adams, 76–77
Roosevelt, F. D., 36
Rosenstock-Huessy, Eugen, 62
Rosetta, 53, 54, 55, 56, 57–58, 59,
    61, 82, 83, 84, 93, 95, 96, 106–
    107, 109–110
Ross, Alan, 75
Huessy-Rosenstock, Eugen, 62

S

Samuels, Andrew, 105
Sawyer, Tom, 2
Scarlett, Liam:
    choreography by, 1, 91–96,
        106–107
    portraying Rosetta's
        soliloquy, 110

typology in, 116–117
Schwartz, Delmore, 75
Sea and the Mirror, The (Auden), 27, 50
Sensation (Emble), 53, 55, 57, 93, 95
"September 1, 1939", 8, 23, 24, 107
"Seven Ages, The" (*The Age of Anxiety*):
    musical adaptation of, 80, 81
    narrative function of, 52, 53–54, 61
    Robbins' choreography of, 87
    Scarlett's choreography of, 93–94
Shadow:
    Auden's Lame Shadow, 43
    imagery used by Auden of, 42
    problem of collective, 48–49
Shakespeare, William, 27–28, 53–54
Shawn, Allen, 84, 85
"Shoes That Were Danced to Pieces, The" (Grimm brothers), 128
Shorter, Bani, 105
Sieg im Westen, 23
Simeone, Nigel, 76, 77
Soldiers, 128–134
Spain (Auden), 17
Spanish Civil War, 17, 22
Spender, Stephen, 22, 46, 47, 79
"Sportsmen, The" (Auden), 21
Stadier paa Livensvegt (Kierkegaard), 60
Standard Edition of the Complete Psychological Works (Freud), 43
Steps to An Ecology of Mind (Bateson), 11
Stern, James, 11, 13, 29
Stossel, Scott, 1, 112–113, 116–117
Sturluson, Snorri, 131
"Summer Night, A" (Auden), 16
Superior function, 47
Symbols of Transformation (Jung), 43
Symphony No. 2 (Bernstein):

creation and structure of, 79–80
critical response to, 84–86
"Dirge, The", 80, 81–82
"Epilogue", 83, 84
Finale, 84
"Masque, The", 80, 81–83
Neumeier's choreography of, 90–91
premiere of, 81, 83
"Prologue", 80
revised ending of, 84
Robbins' choreography of, 87–90
Scarlett's choreography of, 91–96

T

Tales of Grimm and Andersen (Auden), 45
Temenos, 51, 63
Tempest (Shakespeare), 27–28
Terry, Walter, 89
Thinking (Malin), 53, 55, 56, 57, 58–59, 61, 81, 83, 86, 93, 95–96, 109
"Three Snake Leaves, The" (Grimm brothers), 128
Tillich, Paul, 41, 110
Times Literary Supplement, 75
Tobias, Roy, 87, 88
Tolkien, J.R.R., 116
Toller, Ernst, 42
Tristan and Isolde (Wagner), 10
Two Essays on Analytical Psychology (Jung), 42
Typology:
    artistic inspiration in, 106, 116–117
    Auden's self-descriptions, 45, 46–47
    Bernstein's use of, 78–79, 84–85
    character pairings by, 55–56

design of *Age of Anxiety*
emphasizing, 60–61
Extraverted Feeling type, 84–85
Feeling-Sensation type, 44
Hardy's, 44–45
Introverted Thinking type, 110
Introverted Thinking-Intuitive
type, 44, 45, 61–62, 84, 114
Introverted Thinking-Sensation
type, 47–48
Jung's theory of, 56, 61, 107
Kallman's characteristics, 47–48
literary value of, 107
reflected in Robbins'
choreography, 89–90
represented by protagonists, 53
Scarlett's interpretation of,
94–96
shadow imagery, 42, 43
use by Auden, 43–44, 53, 103–
104, 107

U

*Understanding and Treating Anxiety
Disorders* (Wolfe), 112–113
Une saison en enfer (Rimbaud), 25

V

Verse. *See* Poetry
Viehmann, Dorothea, 128
Von Arnim, Friedmund, 128

W

"W. H. Auden Speaks of Poetry and
Total War" (*Chicago Sun*), 28–29
Wagner, Richard, 10
"Wanderer, The" (Auden), 15
War:
Auden's part in Spanish Civil,
17–18
Auden's poems about, 24–25, 108
berserker soldiers in, 131–134

commentary on poetry and,
28–29
defining anxiety in time of,
50–51
effect on consciousness, 4
folk tales about, 128–134
influencing Auden's identity,
7–8, 12
War and the Poet review by Auden, 7
"Watershed, The" (Auden), 13
Wirth, Stacy, 82–83
Wolfe, Dr. Barry E., 112–113
Wood, Jane, 91
World of Man, The (Groddeck), 43
World Within World (Spender), 79

Y

Yeats, W. B., 8, 22, 23, 107
Young-ah Gottlieb, Susannah, 60–61

Z

Zwicky, Jan, 104–105

ABOUT THE AUTHOR

C raig Stephenson Ph.D., is a graduate of the C. G. Jung Institute Zürich, the Institute for Psychodrama, Zumikon, and the Centre for Psychoanalytic Studies, University of Essex. He is a Jungian analyst in private practice in New York City. His books include *Possession: Jung's Comparative Anatomy of the Psyche* (Routledge, 2009) and *Anteros: A Forgotten Myth* (Routledge, 2011). He edited a collection of essays, *Jung and Moreno: Essays on the Theatre of Human Nature* (Routledge, 2014) and a previously unpublished lecture by Jung: *On Psychological and Visionary Art: Jung's Lecture on Gérard de Nerval's "Aurélia"* (2015) for the Philemon Foundation and Princeton University Press. He is Director of Training of the Jungian Psychoanalytic Association, New York City.

Lightning Source UK Ltd.
Milton Keynes UK
UKOW05f0609141116

287531UK00002B/35/P